This textbook is dedicated to
James P. Greenan, Ph.D.

TRAINING DESIGN

FOR THE

HOSPITALITY INDUSTRY

Christine Jaszay, Ph.D. • *Paul Dunk*

THOMSON

DELMAR LEARNING

Australia Canada Mexico Singapore Spain United Kingdom United States

THOMSON
DELMAR LEARNING

Training Design for the Hospitality Industry
by Christine Jaszay and Paul Dunk

Vice President, Career Education
Strategic Business Unit:
Dawn Gerrain

Director of Editorial:
Sherry Gomoll

Senior Acquisitions Editor:
Joan M. Gill

Editorial Assistant:
Lisa Flatley

Director of Production:
Wendy A. Troeger

Production Manager :
Carolyn Miller

Production Editor:
Matthew J. Williams

Director of Marketing:
Donna J. Lewis

Channel Manager:
Wendy E. Mapstone

Cover Image:
Getty Images

For permission to use material from this text or product, contact us by
Tel   (800) 730-2214
Fax   (800) 730-2215
www.thomsonrights.com

Library of Congress Cataloging-in-Publication Data

Jaszay, Christine.
      Training design for the hospitality industry /
Christine Jaszay, Paul Dunk.
         p. cm.
Includes bibliographical references and index.
      ISBN 0-7668-4593-1
   1. Hospitality industry--Study and teaching.
   2. Hospitality industry--Employees--Training of.
   I. Dunk, Paul. II. Title.
      TX911.5.J37 2003
      647.94'071--dc21
                                          2003008415

NOTICE TO THE READER

Table of Contents

Preface   x

CHAPTER 1   **INTRODUCTION TO TRAINING**   1
Formal vs. Informal Training   4
Diversity of the Workforce   6
Review of Marketing and Standards   7
Human Resources Management Review   10

CHAPTER 2   **TRAINING DESIGN MODEL**   15
The Training Design Model   16
Needs Assessment   17
The Training Plan   17
Lesson Plans   18
Train-the-Trainer   19
Training Implementation and Evaluation   20
Coaching and Counseling   20
Case Study   21
Summary of the Model   24

CHAPTER 3   **NEEDS ASSESSMENT PLANNING**   27
Planning Considerations   27
Types of Needs Assessments   28
Needs Assessment Methods   29
Existing Documents   31
Needs Assessment is Common Sense   31
Employee Input in Needs Assessment   32

CHAPTER 4   **IMPLEMENTING NEEDS ASSESSMENT**   41
Interviews and Questionnaires   42
Interviews   42
Questionnaires   44

Questionnaire Development Checklist   45
Prepare Employees for Needs Assessment   50

CHAPTER 5   **PLANNING JOB ANALYSIS**   54

Instructional Design   54
Job Lists   55
Work Simplification and Motion Economy   58
Principles of Work Simplification   60

CHAPTER 6   **IMPLEMENTING JOB ANALYSIS**   67

Job List   68
Categorize Job List   71
Task Analysis   73

CHAPTER 7   **TRAINING METHODS AND ADULT LEARNING
            PRINCIPLES**   82

How Adults Learn   82
Training Methods   85
The Demonstration Method   86
Simulations   87
Role Plays   88
Lectures   88
Self-Instructional Activities   89
Classroom Methods   89
Prepared Training Materials   90
On-the-Job Training   90

CHAPTER 8   **TRAINING PLAN**   96

Define the Trainees   96
Training Objectives   99
Selecting the Trainer   102
Determining the Training Schedule   104

CHAPTER 9   **LESSON PLANS**   112

Do You Really Need To Go Through All Of
This To Turn On The Oven?   118

CHAPTER 10   **GROUP TRAINING AND TEAM-BUILDING**   129

Training Diverse Employees   132
Training Disabled Employees   133
Group Dynamics and Team-building   134
Team-building Strategies   135

CHAPTER 11   **TRAIN-THE-TRAINER**   145

Train-The-Trainer Instruction   145
Trainer Characteristics   146
Design Train-The-Trainer Instruction   147
Demonstration Critique Form   162

CHAPTER 12   **IMPLEMENTING TRAINING AND EVALUATION**   165

Utilizing the Training Documents   166
Mastering the Training   166
The Four Levels of Evaluation   168
Test Criteria   170
Evaluation Instruments or Activities   171
Training Critique Form   174
Cost of Training   175

CHAPTER 13   **COACHING AND COUNSELING**   178

Motivation   178
Diversity   180
Communication   181
Supervision   184

CHAPTER 14   **COSTING THE TRAINING PROGRAM**   190

Cost Determination Before or After   190
Cost of Training Design versus Cost of Training   191
Cost Analysis Form   192
The Garden Terrace Inn: Determining the Cost of Training Design   194

Glossary   197
Index   203

Preface

Training Design for the Hospitality Industry is written for both hospitality managers and students to demonstrate the art of training design. As professionals, we acknowledge the importance of training, but many of us have never actually experienced it ourselves. Suffice it to say that it would be difficult to teach formal training when we may not even recognize it. This textbook solves that problem. By the end of the book, you will be dreaming about "needs assessment," "task analysis," and other things you may never have considered before.

"Instructional Design" is a degree option in university education programs, although it is rarely taught outside these formats. Very few hospitality schools teach how to design training (even though well-designed training is recognized as essential for the success of hospitality operations). This book is written to provide much needed instruction to industry professionals.

As a young person, I worked most restaurant positions at one time or another. I was trained to cook, serve, and host, mostly by trailing employees already doing those particular jobs. Later, as Food Service Director for an existing operation, my staff trained new employees by leading them around a shift or two until they could do the jobs themselves. In addition, I conducted in-service training each month. An earlier interest in theater helped me approach these in-service days as if I was putting on a "show." I wrote a script and had things planned so I would not look like an idiot. As far as I could tell, it worked! Usually my staff enjoyed the in-services, and I liked doing them as well.

After that success, the company asked me to be on the opening team for a new facility. I was excited about the opportunity and the challenge. I determined the menus and designed and set up the systems of operation for food service. I wrote job descriptions and hired new staff, and it was at that point I realized there was nobody to follow around in training.

Everything was new, and everyone was a rookie. I had no idea how to train them before opening to the public.

I am not sure how we did it, but we opened. There was a multitude of problems, though, and I dealt with each and every one in the course of my *18-hour days.*

I opened the food service department of a much bigger and more complex operation a year later. I had learned a lot, but it was still chaos. It was some time after recuperation that I decided there had to be a better way to train employees. I enrolled at Purdue University and pursued two graduate degrees (with minors in instructional design) to learn everything there was about the field. My goal was to pass this knowledge on to hospitality students, because I felt training design was essential and that people were presently not being taught.

I have tried to distill knowledge from my six years of graduate school instructional design study (and several years teaching training design) into a practical "how-to" guide that hospitality managers can apply to their own facilities' training needs. I also have provided them with a means for figuring out exactly what those needs are. Training design is not difficult. It is, however, very time consuming and somewhat tedious. We can use common sense, though, once we are attuned to the sequential steps that turn training design into a manageable process.

I discovered that my scripting idea for conducting in-service training was not really so far off. I was unaware at the time that I could use the same concept for designing on-the-job type training. I have outlined the steps and provided examples so that you can apply common sense when designing the particular system you need. Training design consultants are available to design programs, but as managers we can do it ourselves at a fraction of the cost. It is not that hard, and this book shows you how.

How To Use This Text

Training Design for the Hospitality Industry can serve as the basis for a college course in training design, or it can be used by hospitality managers to guide them through the design process for their own facilities. College students may best be taught with a corresponding class project. I have had success acting as a training consultant, leading my staff (students in training class) through the design of training for real operations. Different classes undertook different projects. Housekeeper, front desk agent, server, intern, and food service manager, for instance, were all positions for which my classes designed training. Local hotels and restaurants are often very happy to have a class design free training for them.

This text may be used to provide information and written examples that students will be utilizing in their class projects. While the focus of the text is on actual design, background information is presented as appropriate for their education. Practitioners, on the other hand, may wish to move directly to the "how-to" chapters and use examples as a model or pattern for their own design. However you choose to use the text, though, my hope is that you find it helpful.

Acknowledgments

Delmar Learning and the authors would like to thank the following reviewers for the valuable feedback that they provided:

Robert M. O'Halloran, Ph.D.
    State University of New York at Plattsburgh

Glenn Baron
    TBG

Elaine Madden
    Anne Arundel Community College

G. Michael Harris
    Bethune-Cookman College

Dan Crafts
    S. W. Missouri State University

K. Virginia Hemby, Ph.D.
    Indiana University of Pennsylvania

1 Introduction to Training

OBJECTIVES

The purpose of this chapter is to define and describe training and its importance to an organization. A review of marketing and human resource management is also covered.

Upon completion of Chapter 1 the student should be able to

- Describe the difference between formal and informal training and discuss why formal training is more effective.

- Define turnover and its negative impacts on an organization. Consider possible solutions.

- Describe workforce demographics and how this affects management and training.

- Define illiteracy and its implications for hospitality management.

- Define and discuss marketing, focusing on the origin of standards.

- Describe the job of management in relation to the human resource model.

- Describe components of the human resource model, and discuss the relationship between training and other components of the model.

Introduction to Training

Training is the process used for the development of knowledge and skills needed to perform the jobs, duties, and tasks found in an organization. This process, in most cases, involves supervising new employees while they perform the job for a shift or two, then standing back and unleashing them on an unsuspecting public. As they gradually improve through a process of trial and error, the customer suffers and so does business. We may have heard servers say, "Please, bear with me. This is my first day on the job."

Okay, imagine shopping for a new car. The dealer lets it slip about how the manufacturer had new people on the assembly line the day they put that car together. Perhaps they were the ones in charge of welding bucket seats down. People who were taken right off the street and handed a soldering gun. How heavily would the idea of the car's floor falling off weigh on your mind? Maybe it would happen later while you were out riding on the interstate. Nothing but blue sky and a couple puffy clouds above, when suddenly there is a great tearing sound at your feet. Next thing you know, you have run over yourself.

With that in mind, would you buy the car?

The hospitality industry is a service industry. We may prepare food or clean rooms, but *service* is the real product. We serve meals, or we provide lodging for our guests. Service and product are so closely intertwined that service becomes the product. Thus, if service is lacking because of inexperienced or poorly trained employees, customers are paying for a product and not getting it. It is our responsibility to make sure that all customers get exactly what they are supposed to get, every time. Consistency, in a word. If we do not take that responsibility seriously, thereby assuring our customers' satisfaction, they will promptly go elsewhere.

This is an extremely competitive industry. Consider the number of restaurants and hotels that are available in the vicinity of your own home. In the Phoenix metro area there are 355 hotels and 9,019 restaurants servicing a population of 3,192,125. In Flagstaff, just two hours away, 57,700 residents may choose from 53 hotels and 215 restaurants. What's to keep customers loyal but quality service and product? With the current costs of opening and operating a service-oriented business, is there really any room for lameness?

We compete for customers, but likewise, we must also compete for employees. Most of us know which hotels and restaurants are the best employers in our hometowns. We also know which are not very good. **Turnover** is the rate at which businesses replace workers. Every time an employee leaves, another must be hired and trained. If the turnover rate is high, fairly inexperienced employees could be training new ones. So, who trained the employee doing the training? An employee with four months on the job might conceivably have seniority in a hospitality operation with high turnover. Lameness begets lameness.

Some managers of organizations with high turnover rates rationalize that it's the low quality of applicants creating the problem, so, they conclude, spending any money on training is a waste. After all, they will just quit or have to be fired. When this self-fulfilling prophecy comes true, naturally the organization is understaffed, existing staff members are overworked, and they soon get frustrated and quit. The cycle continues. The business gets an aura around it—a pall, as if bankruptcy looms just around the corner. Quality people do not stay at places like that. More employees quit in the first month than at any other time because they may not feel comfortable, competent, or appreciated. Or they may not feel that the business is viable, due to mismanagement.

Operators sell an appealing image of the establishment to customers. They must also sell this image to prospective employees. The establishment must be seen as a good place to be for current and future workers. There is a correlation between satisfied employees and satisfied customers. For customers to return, the service experience must match the advertisement. Likewise, for workers to stay, the work environment must be positive and rewarding. High turnover is generally the fault of management. Either they hired the wrong people to begin with, did not train them adequately, or did not manage their resources (time, money, employees, equipment, etc.) properly. Therefore, it is management's responsibility to head off future problems by starting on the right foot via initiating proper new-hire training systems.

Industries (other than service) consider 25 percent turnover to be excessive. The hospitality industry has turnover rates up to 300 percent. That means that within a year the whole staff will quit and be replaced three times. That's a lot of work. Turnover directly and indirectly affects profit due to search/selection costs, hiring/training costs, separation costs, production losses, waste, and accidents. There is a decrease in morale among existing employees and a subsequent loss in customer base.

Bottom line: Turnover may jeopardize the very survival of the business itself.

Formal vs. Informal Training

We cannot operate successfully with high levels of turnover. It is management's responsibility—our responsibility—to reduce turnover to reasonable rates. **Formal Training** is structured. It follows a predetermined plan of instruction (as opposed to shadowing an employee already doing the job), and has been shown to increase productivity and job satisfaction while reducing turnover. Managers, however, may not know how to construct formal training programs unless they have experienced similar schooling themselves, taken a class in training design, or used a corporate formal training program.

Hands-on learning is probably the most effective delivery method for training the typical entry-level hospitality worker of today. Most college-educated managers have experienced the lecture method of instruction and may lack experience for training employees using hands-on methods. Design of formal in-house training programs can be laborious and tedious. Without technical know-how, managers often opt for unstructured and less effective **Informal Training** (where there is no predetermined written plan).

In the hospitality industry, training is often delivered by experienced workers—people who are experts at the job they are teaching. Therefore, an experienced cook trains a novice cook. A commonly held assumption, though, is that subject matter experts possess instructional knowledge and skills. Some do and some do not. Cooking and teaching someone to cook are not the same and require very different skills. Quality training has proven to be a cost-effective solution for the hospitality industry's problems, yet businesses often relegate training to people who may never have experienced effective training themselves (compounded by their never having received instruction in how to train). Trainers who have not been **trained-to-train** often deliver low quality, ineffective, inefficient, and inconsistent training.

Informal training, where a new employee shadows or follows another employee doing the job, can be effective. Provided the "trainer" happens to be a natural teacher, is patient, isn't too busy, does the job the correct way, and is able to supply answers for questions the new employee might not know to ask. Often times, employees who are working their regular shift (with a new employee in tow) are too busy to take time to explain what they are doing, and why, and (even if they had the time) they might not be capable of clearly explaining the process. They may not have been trained properly to begin with, and, for all management knows, they may not be doing the job the correct or best way.

There is more than one way to train. We are familiar with the idea of new employees following experienced ones, but it might not be the most effective way to teach someone a new skill. It is important that servers be able to answer questions about menu items. Following an experienced server will not necessarily teach the new employee how to answer questions posed by customers. A structured class environment might be better geared for instruction. Perhaps a session with lecture and handouts where menu items could be identified and described. Exercises and role-playing would serve to illustrate the questions new servers might be asked.

It would, of course, be difficult to teach cooking without having subject matter expertise. A washroom attendant isn't really the best instructor to demonstrate the fine art of crepe making. Skilled, experienced employees, however, are a necessary component in any technical training program. Interested and technically skilled employees selected as "trainers" can be taught the technology of teaching that is composed of principles of learning, design of instruction, and teaching methods. Professional *train-the-trainer* instruction enables the novice trainer to approach training design and implementation in a systematic manner. Trainers are taught to identify the overall objectives of a program and to outline the framework for individual lessons and materials. Trainers can also be taught to analyze the target audience and customize instruction for specific learners.

Effective hospitality industry training programs are the result of blending two separate technologies: the technology of teaching, and the technology of industry. The former is derived from the field of education. Hospitality managers are not doing line jobs. They are hiring, training, and supervising employees who do these line jobs. Twenty-five percent of a manager's time may be spent in activities that include orientation and training new hires, additional training for current employees, ongoing coaching, evaluation of training activities, and communicating standards.

Managers must be trained in instructional design and appropriate strategies for adult learners. Industry training is expensive, and without planning and professional instructional design, the program may not be effective, comprehensive, job-specific, cost-effective, consistent, or manageable. Structured training requires less training time, results in a higher level of job competence, decreases production losses, and enables employees to solve more production problems. When training is designed in advance (formal), everything that needs to be taught is included, and every trainee gets the same high quality training.

Managers unfamiliar with instructional design (and who were not formally trained themselves) may be unaware of their deficiencies.

Attainment of competencies through unstructured training may not have been checked, so they might not be aware that the trainee did not reach competency. Perhaps they are satisfied with existing training programs because they do not know any better. Consequently, they will attribute their unmanageable employee turnover and declining quality of service and productivity to the "poor quality of the work pool."

Diversity of the Workforce

Nearly 7.6 million people are employed in the United States hospitality, travel, and tourism industries, and more than 21 percent employment growth is expected for the next five years. These industries are already among the largest employers in 28 states. Sales and customer counts are increasing in hotels and restaurants, but qualified workers are increasingly difficult to recruit and retain. The workforce grew about 2.5 percent annually during the 1980s, 1.2 percent during the 1990s, and its growth is expected to soon drop below 1 percent. We have fewer, less skilled people available . . . for more jobs.

The pool of available workers is changing in several ways. Our country's population is growing more slowly and aging at the same time. Workers between the ages of 35 and 54 are expected to make up 48 percent of the workforce by 2005. People over the age of 55 are and will be available to fill many of the job openings in the hospitality industry. The previous availability of teenagers and young adults for entry-level hospitality jobs is a thing of the past. The stereotypical belief that older workers could not easily learn new skills (and had diminished problem-solving capabilities) has until now inhibited older workers from consideration as a potential labor source.

Women are expected to make up 47.4 percent of the workforce by 2007. Half of the female workers may be "primary" income earners with children under the age of 18. Seventy to eighty percent of the new workers will be women, minorities, and immigrants. It is predicted that the minority population of the U.S. will increase to 47 percent by the year 2050.

Twenty percent of American adults cannot read, write, or compute adequately to be productive workers. Up to half of this group may be totally illiterate. It is estimated that 75 percent of all jobs in the United States require some technical training in a continuing education mode. **Illiteracy** is often hidden and not easily detected, but because of the large numbers of known illiterate and functionally illiterate adults, it is reasonable to expect that many of these people are employed in the hospitality industry and involved in training programs.

Some hospitality companies have begun to question the effectiveness of training programs for illiterate people. To address this problem, they have developed in-house literacy programs that have been shown to increase morale, employee loyalty, and productivity while, at the same time, reducing turnover rates. Some organizations have created self-contained corporate schools to provide employees with specific job skills and/or the continuing education necessary to respond to societal gaps that make training less effective.

Increased immigration has resulted in larger numbers of people learning English as a second language. People with different languages, social customs, standards, and cultural backgrounds are entering the work force in greater numbers. More socially, educationally, and financially disadvantaged people are also entering the work force.

Chronic unemployment and labor shortages are beginning to be addressed in tandem in cities across the country. Hospitality corporations experiencing difficulty in staffing entry-level positions are attempting to produce a pool of skilled workers by seeking the chronically unemployed who are physically able to work. This group is trained in job-specific skills, basic skills, and life skills. Graduates of these training programs are then available for entry-level positions.

Industry and community-related programs are responding to the idea that business and community are directly related; businesses are less likely to be healthy in an unhealthy society. The chronically unemployed and/or homeless, participating in training programs, can expect to experience increased self-esteem and self-confidence. This increased self-esteem, in turn, tends to enable people to become more receptive to training.

Today's workers have increased job expectations and are less willing to be humble and obedient, preferring some latitude, recognition, respect, and input into how the company is managed. Workers are less willing to perform boring jobs and depend on their work for personal fulfillment.

The successful management of an increasingly diverse workforce requires enhanced communication and leadership skills . . . as well as an ability to teach and train individuals with varying degrees of experience and understanding. The focus for management must be on accommodating change, rather than resisting it.

Review of Marketing and Standards

Hospitality is big business. It has become so complex that it is less and less feasible for nonprofessionals to succeed using "seat-of-the-pants" methods.

Let's look at restaurants. Thirty percent fail in their first year, often because their creators naively believed they could succeed through optimism. Being gung-ho alone is only good when you are rooting for the Cubs.

Consider this: After having guests over for a home-cooked dinner, we have maybe heard people say, "You should open a restaurant!" Well, it is not all that difficult to open a restaurant. We can rent a space, some equipment, get some groceries on credit—and "Presto! We're restaurateurs!"

You had better have a lot of friends or a rooftop deck overlooking Wrigley Field.

Willy Loman, in *Death of a Salesman*, said he could "sell anything." Fifty years ago that was possible. Today the business community is far too competitive. If there is only one restaurant in town, people have no choice if they want to go out for a meal. Even small towns now have lots of restaurant choices, though. It is no longer possible to sell people something if it does not specifically meet some need they have. They can simply walk down two doors and find something that better suits them.

Think of all the people who go to restaurants. Are they looking for the same thing? Do we all like the same thing? Hardly. Older professional women might prefer a place that is quiet, well lit, pretty, and specializing in food that is low fat and in small portions. Price may not be a main concern. *Chuck E. Cheese's* or *Peter Piper Pizza* would not be an appealing choice for that particular group. Kids, however, would probably prefer *Chuck E. Cheese's*. One isn't necessarily better than the other. One is, however, a better match for a particular group of customers. *McDonalds* might not be the best choice for a romantic dinner, yet it would be perfect for a quick "bite" on the way to a hockey game.

To be successful in today's competitive marketplace, it is essential we identify who our customers will be. Then we must make sure we are preparing foods and serving them in a suitable way for their specific tastes. A restaurant that tries to please everyone will more than likely fail. Try to imagine a concept that would appeal to young families, teens, college students, young professionals, blue collar workers, older women, rich, poor, young, old, etc. One size does not fit all (despite that myth about *Spandex*), and when customers have choices, they will choose the restaurant, hotel, event, or store that best meets their individual needs.

Marketing identifies customers and then develops products, pricing, and distribution directed at satisfying their needs and wants. Instead of opening a restaurant or hotel and then waiting for customers to show up, we begin with choosing the customers we want to serve. Then we plan the business specifically for them. We design menu items, amenities, prices, location, facilities, and decor they would like. After which we advertise in a way that speaks to our customers. Marketing. Specificity. It is not rocket science.

That having been said, we can come up with the perfect business for specific customers and still fail if we do not consider *uncontrollable variables*. What if there are other restaurants or hotels already doing what we want to do? Are there enough customers in this group to make our establishment successful? What if the other restaurant or hotel owns the building outright, and we have to pay rent or a mortgage? Can we afford to charge the same for menu items as the other place?

We must also ascertain that we have enough money to do what we originally had in mind. If we wanted to serve well-to-do retired people, could we afford the linens, china, flatware, furniture, and facilities they would probably expect? Our wondrous menu won't work if we cannot get ingredients from a supplier consistently. What if we do not have qualified staff to prepare and serve these menu items?

We need to replace our old definition of marketing as "going to the store" or as being synonymous with "selling." A market is not a place to shop. Instead, a market is all the people who, in the case of restaurants, go out to eat. In marketing we divide or **segment** the whole market into smaller groups of people with similar product needs based on commonalties such as age, interests, lifestyles, etc. We then **target** or choose the group that we specifically want to please because we cannot please everyone. We consider all the uncontrollable environments we have to operate within: competition, suppliers, human resources, financial limitations, etc., so that the menu we finally write or the hotel we design is feasible and can be successful.

A **standard** is a clear, concise description of the way something is to be or is to be done. Most standards in hospitality operations are based on the way our targeted customers want things done. We have a diverse workforce, though, with prospective employees who might have entirely different standards from those of our customers. A twenty-three-year-old male server in a tearoom geared toward women would most likely have different standards in terms of food preferences, portion sizes, decor, and background music (*Pantera* and tea do not mix).

Management is responsible for assuring that customer-desired standards are met and maintained. This requires consistent, effective formal training to enable all our employees to meet the same standards. It also requires ongoing coaching and training of employees so as to consistently maintain the standards our customers expect and demand. It will not happen by chance, and if customers are not satisfied, they will go elsewhere.

Human Resources Management Review

Formal training can enable employees to meet and maintain standards of the operation. It is almost always better than informal training. However, to be most effective, it is essential that we hire the right people for the job. For employees to be successful, three things are necessary: They must want to do the job, they must be capable of doing the job, and they must be shown *how* to do the job. Someone who is out of work and needs a job, but who does not really want to do the job, will lose interest as soon as something else comes along. Someone who doesn't have the capabilities to do the job will not be able to be effectively trained. A person who really wants to do the job and is capable may not do the job correctly if he or she has not been properly trained.

Employees serve guests. The manager's job is to make the operation work by hiring appropriate staff and training, supervising, and evaluating their performance. Training is just one component in a human resources model, and all components together make for successful staffing. Let's review a human resources model:

Job Analysis

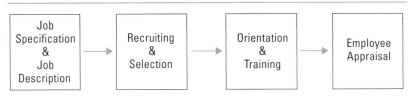

The point is to hire the right people for the job. In other words, people who have the characteristics and/or skills that match those necessary to be successful. To be able to select these people requires **recruiting** the appropriate applicants. Basically, finding them and letting them know the job is available. **Job Specifications** and **Job Descriptions** are tools we use to recruit and select employees for available positions. A job specification describes the characteristics, skills, education, and experience the person needs for the position. They must have these traits to be hired. In fact, they should have them—as far as we can tell—to even be interviewed. Time is money. The job description describes the position and lists the main duties the person will be required to perform after training. We **select** the person who best matches the job specification and description by reviewing applications and conducting interviews.

Hiring appropriate people for specific positions may be the most important task facing managers. Job specifications and descriptions must accurately describe the person and the position because they are used in selection as the basis for hiring. If they are not accurate, we could hire someone who matches the documents but not the real position. Then we will be trying to train someone who might not be capable. **Job Analysis** is the rigorous research process we utilize to update or write accurate job specifications and descriptions. We ask those doing the particular position what exactly it is they do. We also watch them do the job to see whether what they actually do matches what they say they do. We ask managers and/or other employees what they think the duties of the position are. We can see what similar operations have their people doing in that position. If everyone agrees, that's our job description. If the information varies from source to source, we figure out what is real and necessary for the employee to do in that position to meet the needs of our customers. At the same time we can be asking and watching for the qualifications necessary to be able to do the job successfully. That becomes the job specification.

Once the best match for the position has been selected, the new employee is instructed to report for work. The employee's first day on the job sets the tone for that person's relationship with the company. Most turnover occurs in the first month of employment. **Orientation** is where we introduce and welcome new employees into the fold. When we have guests in our home we try to make them comfortable. We do the same for new employees. We let them know what they are to wear, when they are supposed to arrive, through what door they should enter, whether they should bring food for themselves, and so forth. We greet them at the door, show them around, and try to make them feel comfortable. We explain the rules and what appropriate behavior is expected. We may go over policies, benefits, and company history at this time. **Training** teaches new employees how to do the job they were hired for. Orientation and training allow employees to assimilate faster and more successfully into the organization and to be more effective employees.

Employees learn how to do the job to the standards in training. **Supervision** is the ongoing day-to-day monitoring of the employees' performance with reinforcement and corrective feedback to maintain standards achieved in training. **Employee Appraisal** is a formal periodic interview with individual employees to discuss specific job performance strengths and weaknesses for the purpose of improving performance. There are no service encounters without employees. The quality of service is contingent on management's effective utilization of the tools in the human resources model.

The focus of this text is on the training component, but all components are necessary, as each component is dependent on the others.

CONCLUSION

Intense competition has forced the hospitality industry to become more pro-oriented. Traditional advancement through the ranks has become less common as hospitality organizations have recruited college graduates for management track positions. "Seat-of-the-pants" management practices have given way to more effective methods derived from analysis of successful operations. Diversity of the workforce, illiteracy, labor shortages, and increased competition have made formal training a necessity to decrease turnover and meet customer expectations.

KEY WORDS

Training	Recruiting
Turnover	Job Specification
Formal Training	Job Description
Informal Training	Selection
Illiteracy	Job Analysis
Marketing	Orientation
Segment	Supervision
Target Market	Employee Appraisal
Standard	

CHAPTER THOUGHT QUESTIONS

1. Describe how you were trained for each of the different jobs you have held in the past. Describe the difference between formal and informal training, and identify whether your training experiences have been formal or informal. How could your training have been improved?

2. Describe the turnover rate at your current or past jobs. Could the rate be reduced? How? Why is it better for companies to have lower turnover rates? What is an acceptable turnover rate?

3. Identify the various diverse groups that were represented by the employees at a current or previous job you have held. Describe the diversity you may expect to experience on your staff when you are a manager.

4. Define illiteracy and discuss problems that could arise in a hospitality department if there were one or more unidentified illiterate staff members. How might you identify illiterate staff, and what can you do about it?

5. Why must hospitality operations today have a "marketing" orientation rather than a "sales" orientation? How do the two orientations differ?

6. Identify the target market at your last or current job. What did the operation do to meet the specific desires of the target market? Describe the product, the place, the promotion, and the pricing.

7. Describe the manager's job in terms of the human resources model, and compare it to the way managers you have worked for did the job.

8. One of the duties of managers is hiring staff. Discuss the three necessary factors for a potential employee to be a successful hire. How did a current or previous manager you have worked for hire staff? Did he or she make sure new employees have the three essential factors? What was the result?

9. What is a standard? Where does the standard come from? Whose standard is it? Can the standard vary? Discuss standards in terms of marketing and human resource management.

10. The hospitality industry is very competitive. Discuss competition in terms of customers and employee recruiting and retention and how it affects hospitality organizations.

REFERENCES

Billions of dollars and millions of jobs. (2000). *Tourism Works For America 2000, Ninth Edition.* 8–23.

Cothran, C. C., & Combrink, T. E. (1999). Attitudes of minority adolescents toward hospitality industry careers. *Hospitality Management, 18,* 143–158.

Goldberg, B. (1997). Future workforce. *Executive-Excellence, 14*(12), 4.

Greengard, S. (1998). Five myths of today's labor market. *Workforce, 77*(3), 48.

Harvey, B. H. (1999) Technology, diversity and work culture: Key trends in the next millennium. *HRMagazine, 44*(11), 58–59.

Larson, M. (1998). Tackling worker illiteracy. *Quality, 37*(11), 42–45.

Whelan-Berry, K. S., & Gordon, J. R. (2000). Strengthening human resource strategies: Insights from the experiences of mid-career professional women. *Human Resource Planning, 23*(1), 26–37.

2 *Training Design Model*

OBJECTIVES

Designing formal training is time-consuming and expensive. Once it is designed, however, it needs updating only as operational changes are instituted. Every new employee may then be trained using the training plan and all materials that are already prepared. There is an initial investment of time and money, of course, but thereafter training is consistent and convenient. The idea is similar to management delegating certain responsibilities. It is usually faster to just "do it myself" than to take the time and energy to show someone else how to do it. However, once the initial effort has been expended, the employee can take the delegated responsibility and free the manager for other tasks. Many employees excel when given opportunities to take on more responsibility. And so with formal training—it better prepares an employee to do the job and, after the initial effort of design, is ready and available for use every time a new employee joins the team.

The purpose of this chapter is to present and describe the model for training design which will be utilized throughout the remainder of the text. The importance and use of models is discussed along with who will use the model in an operation interested in designing formal training. A thorough conceptual understanding of the model will facilitate learning how to develop components of the model later in the text.

Upon completion of Chapter Two, the student should be able to

- Describe and define all components of the training design model.

- Discuss why models are important and useful in training design.

- Discuss how the model is used and who uses the model.

The Training Design Model

Try to imagine baking a cake without a recipe, making a dress without a pattern, or building a house without a plan. Would they turn out the way we envisioned? Perhaps. Perhaps not. Recipes, patterns, or architectural drawings assure us that the finished product will turn out the way it is supposed to. If directions are followed exactly, there should be no difference in the end product no matter which baker prepares the cake. A **model** is a recipe or pattern that when followed results in a desired outcome.

Training is job specific rather than generic, so the end results will not look the same for every job or operation. However, a model is useful as a means of organizing efforts to result in a desired outcome for a particular situation. We have all been taught the scientific method: Define the problem, determine possible solutions, try a solution, try another one if the first one did not solve the problem. That is basically a problem-solving model. We have steps we can take intellectually that can lead us to an answer. Before coming to the model, we may have had a problem and reacted to it before even knowing what the problem was. Our reaction may or may not have had a positive effect.

We do not want to waste time and money designing training and find out later that we still have a problem. The idea is to approach training design intelligently and systematically in order to save time, money, and frustration. And that is the purpose of the model—to give us a step-by-step process which will result in a desired outcome.

The **Training Design Model** is made up of seven interrelated components within the Human Resource Model reviewed in Chapter One. It is a process that meets with employees in the fifth step (with implementation of the training program) and follows through with ongoing coaching and counseling.

Step #1	#2	#3	#4	#5	#6	#7
Needs Assessment	Training Plan	Lesson Plans	Trainer Training	Training Implementation	Training Evaluation	Coaching & Counseling

Training design takes specialized skills. Oftentimes corporations will employ instructional designers to produce training programs for their individual units. If there are no corporate training programs available, general managers will be responsible for training. The purpose of this text is to teach managers, potential managers, or anyone who has training responsibilities in the hospitality industry to design training professionally.

Needs Assessment

The first step in the Training Design Model is the **needs assessment**. This is similar to the first step in the scientific method where we define the problem. In training, as in the scientific method, we want to cut out guesswork and not waste resources on solutions that might not be feasible. Training is not the solution to all problems. Perhaps a problem is the result of hiring mistakes and no amount of training is going to change that fact. Perhaps a change in work schedules, shifts, or supervisors, or any number of things, could solve the problem. We cannot tell how to solve a problem if we do not know precisely what the problem is to begin with.

To throw training at all problems would be fruitless. Problems generally need to be solved in a timely way, though. If one possible solution does not work, another will have to be tried. All of these attempts take time, energy, and money. Needs assessment is the systematic process we use to rigorously collect appropriate data to determine the precise problem and whether or not training is a good fix. If training is a good solution for a particular problem, our needs assessment then involves determining specific training needs. We define the employees needing training so that we will be able to match our training to their particular learning styles, and we write objectives for the training program.

Objectives are statements of what trainees will be able to do upon completion of the training. They are job-specific and behavioral. In other words, action verbs. We say that our trainees will be able to "describe" to guests how menu items are prepared—not "know" how menu items are prepared. Knowing is nice, but we need our servers to *do* something: describe the items. That is a subtle but huge difference in training design. We plan all of our instruction to that outcome. If we want to make sure trainees know how menu items are prepared, we could give them a written or oral test. If, however, we want to know if they can describe the preparation of the menu items to guests, our test would perhaps be a simulation of a server/guest interaction. Knowing and describing are not the same.

The Training Plan

Once we know who and what we are going to train, then we need a plan. The **training plan** is a well-thought-out written plan detailing training topics and a schedule of when, where, and by whom they will be presented. Every step through the training design model is time-consuming. But, once each step is completed, the documents are ready for use whenever called for. A newly hired employee is plugged into this training plan, and there is no wasted time spent trying to figure out how, what, when, and where the employee will be trained.

We would probably never bother designing formal training if we have a small family-run operation with no turnover. If, however, our operation is big, and we have many employees, formal training saves a tremendous amount of time and effort. We do not have to redesign the wheel every single time we have a new employee. Instead, we simply look at the training plan, tell the employee when to show up, review the materials, make sure everything is in place, and, as a result, have excellent training with everything covered in the best way possible.

Lesson Plans

Lesson plans are the most time-consuming and important part of instructional design. Lesson plans are the instruction. A lesson plan is like a recipe that any cook could follow with similar outcomes. Any capable trainer could review a good lesson plan and administer training. Styles and comfort levels vary with experience, but the training would be the same. A **lesson plan** is a training script with all materials, activities, and instructions needed to meet objectives.

Training topics are determined for the training plan from the data collected in needs assessment. There is a lesson plan for each training topic which includes the objective for the particular topic presented (what the trainee is expected to do upon completion of the session). We determine the most effective way to meet the objective. There are many instructional methods available. A lecture is one method, but would probably not be the best method for teaching someone how to work algebraic equations. Working through equations on a chalkboard while explaining the steps and then having students practice these steps, might be a more effective method than lecturing.

Demonstration is often an excellent method for training people how to do something physical such as mopping a floor or cleaning a sink. Showing servers prepared menu items and having them taste the items (while describing ingredients and preparation methods) might be a more effective vehicle for learning about the menu than telling a new server to take the menu home and memorize it or having them watch another server take orders. Training is different than education. In training everyone must get an 'A.' Average is okay in education, but 70 percent positive service encounters, 70 percent properly cooked meals, 70 percent smooth guest check-ins . . . that is not okay. In our highly competitive industry, 30 percent dissatisfied customers will most likely result in bankruptcy.

The objective of each lesson is to be attained at a particular standard level. Standards are generally based on the needs and desires of the target market (our customers). The objectives must be attained by all trainees. We cannot just flunk a trainee who does not get it. It is our responsibility to make sure everyone gets it and gets it entirely, so we choose methods that will enable all trainees to attain objectives at the level of the standards.

Kindergarten through high school teachers are trained to teach. Not all college teachers have received teachers' training. Thus, we may have experienced teachers in college who were not very good teachers. They were smart and knew their subject matter, but they did not seem to know how to get it across very effectively. Lesson planning skill is not something with which we are born. Teachers are taught to develop lesson plans. To be effective, trainers must also have good lesson plans.

Train-the-Trainer

Developing lesson plans is just one of the skills needed to be an effective trainer. We know that all jobs and all people are not the same. Certain characteristics are better matched with certain jobs. If employees do not have the ability and willingness to do a job, we will have limited success in training them to be effective in the position. Just as not everyone has the makeup to be a good server, not everyone can be a good teacher or trainer. Not everyone is willing to train. So we select employees who are willing and capable of training, and then we must train them to train.

Training an employee requires completely different skills from those necessary to do the job. Understanding and utilizing adult learning principles and motivation theory, team-building and communication skills, plus leadership ability all are necessary to be an effective trainer. We must select trainers who are capable of learning this material and developing skills in each of the areas. We have all experienced the difference a good teacher makes in determining how well we learn something. Likewise with training, a good trainer (someone who is willing and capable, and trained-to-train) can make a big difference in the quality of instruction which then positively affects service quality, turnover, and professionalism.

Training Implementation and Evaluation

We design training to be implemented easily and with great success. As with most things, however, practice makes perfect. The first time around, training may not go as smoothly as hoped. The key is to have a good training plan, be well prepared (having gone over the materials in advance), and then be prepared to modify the plan when necessary. Real life often differs from a written plan. The second time through is usually better.

Needs assessment is front-end evaluation. We ask, "What do we need to do?" We design it and do it, and then need to ask, "How did it work?" We use information collected during evaluation to modify and improve the training program. If our needs assessment was thorough, we can be assured that our training needs were correct. It's harder to evaluate something if we have nothing to compare it to. All components of the training design model are interrelated. Managers without professional training may have an undefined problem and throw training at it, only to discover later that something is still wrong. Professionals have the knowledge and skills necessary to identify specific problems, then design appropriate training to meet the objective that alleviates them.

The difference between before and after training is measured to ascertain whether a problem has been alleviated and to what degree. A mini needs assessment is done to determine what modifications may be in order to improve the training's effectiveness. Needs assessment and evaluation are very similar except needs assessment is conducted beforehand to determine if and what training is necessary. **Evaluation** utilizes rigorous research methods and takes place after training to gauge whether or not it was effective.

Coaching and Counseling

Hospitality managers are responsible for seeing that everything happens at the right time and as our guests expect. Our job involves hiring appropriate people for all positions, training them, and supervising them. As defined in Chapter One, supervision is the ongoing day-to-day monitoring of the employees' performance with reinforcement and corrective feedback to maintain standards achieved in training. **Coaching** is a training term for supervision. Essentially, they are the same thing. Coaching/supervision is ongoing training designed to maintain standards, and make sure everyone is doing what they are supposed to be doing.

Old-style authoritarian management is not effective with today's workforce. Employees do not respond well to orders backed up with threats. Coaching may have a more positive connotation than supervision. Today's effective supervision is coaching—monitoring, praising, and positively correcting employees' performance. Formal employee appraisal is done once or twice a year. Coaching is ongoing. There should be no surprises at the formal employee appraisal interview. Performance problems must be corrected immediately. Dissatisfied customers do not return, and constitute a scathing word-of-mouth advertisement.

Morale is improved when management assures that everyone continues to meet standards. For employees who do a good job and care about their work, it can be very annoying and demoralizing to work with others whose poor performance is condoned by management. There are times when performance declines due to personal problems. Most of us have or will experience personal problems that can negatively affect our work. Divorce, death, drug/alcohol addiction, illness, etc., touch many of us and can interrupt our normal functioning.

We are in business, though, and standards must be met no matter what. However, management should be prepared to recognize employees' personal problems and refer them to sources that can help them through their situation. Some employees simply need to know we care and are concerned. They may need some time off to deal with problems. None of us are immune to life's unpleasant surprises, and management may be better served by replacing judgment with compassion and guidance.

It is cost-effective to help employees return to productivity rather than fire them and start over with new employees. We are not trained psychologists and should not attempt to handle serious problems. We should, however, make sure employees get the help they need. We need to recognize warning signs and deal with problems before they become major and affect the operation. It is the right thing to do, and it is good business.

Case Study

The training design model is a set of instructions we can follow to design training for any line position in the hospitality industry. The remaining chapters in the text will focus on components of the training design model, and, as we go through chapters, we will design training for a fictitious sixty-room, full-service hotel called *The Garden Terrace Inn* (GTI). Its target market is upper middle class professionals who desire quiet, safe, and pleasant surroundings . . . and, excellent service.

GTI is located in Chelsea, Arizona, in the midst of lovely gardens overlooking Oak Creek just 20 minutes from Chelsea International Airport. The *Living Room* welcomes guests with well-stocked library shelves, comfortable overstuffed chairs, and a large stone fireplace. Guests and visitors feel at-home in this country inn atmosphere. The *Terrace Lounge* is adjacent to the Living Room and provides beautiful garden views while offering a wide choice of refreshing libations.

A breakfast buffet featuring fresh fruits and home-baked pastries, along with cooked-to-order eggs, is served every morning in the *Garden Room*. Weather permitting, a wall of French doors can be opened ushering in the soothing sounds of nature: Oak Creek, birds, and softly rustling leaves. Luncheon is served either inside or on a series of wrought iron tables with matching chairs on the flagstone patio. Chef Paul prepares healthful, eye-catching dishes selected to delight our guests' palates and please their sensibilities. Later, the Garden Room is filled with fresh flowers and ablaze with candles for our guests' evening dining pleasure. There are separate lunch and dinner menus, as well as daily specials to go along with each.

GTI has state-of-the-art audio/visual equipment and conference facilities perfect for small groups. The garden patio is enchanting for weddings or special events. Amenities provided in each guest room include a TV, small refrigerator, BOSE radio, and Internet access. There is a safe at the front desk for guests' valuables, and, for a small charge, housekeeping will take care of their dry cleaning needs. GTI provides agreeable accommodations for business travel or just an appealing time-out from today's hectic routine.

GTI is independently owned and has been in operation six years. In the past, new hires were trained by other employees and management; but, as business stabilized, ownership determined there was a need for a more effective, efficient, and consistent training program. We are going to approach the training design model as an imaginary *consulting firm* hired by GTI—designing imaginary training—for an imaginary inn.

The Garden Terrace Inn Organizational Chart

General Manager: Jim Charles, 42, was hired six years ago to open and manage GTI. He has a bachelor's degree in liberal arts and for many years was food and beverage manager for a large, successful hotel in San Francisco. His experience, combined with a refreshing

The Garden Terrace Inn

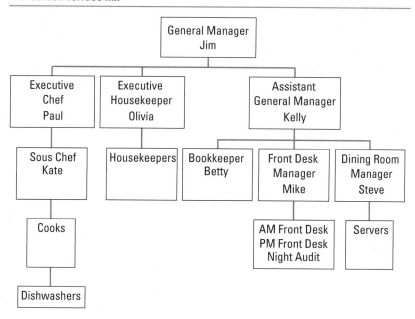

vision for the inn, convinced owner Frank Stranten that Jim could make his business a success.

Jim compensated for his lack of comprehensive experience by hiring excellent people in top management positions. His emphasis is on GTI as a team. He allows his support staff autonomy (with guidance) to assure that the needs of the target market are met. His management style is courteous, caring, and professional.

Assistant General Manager: Kelly McKay, 35, has been with Jim since opening. She has worked nearly every job in the hotel business over the past eighteen years. Her last position was Front Desk Manager at the elegant Bennett Arms downtown. She felt that her lack of formal education, however, was limiting her career and believed that GTI offered more responsibility, autonomy, and potential.

Front Desk Manager: Mike Francis, 28, has a degree in elementary education but grew tired of teaching after three years in the profession. He worked front desk at two major hotels before coming to GTI. He supervises the morning and evening front desk employees and the night auditor.

Dining Room Manager: Steve Edwards, 34, will receive his engineering degree next year. He began waiting tables at GTI when he went back to school four years ago. He has been supervising servers the past two years.

Bookkeeper: Betty Duncan, 57, worked as C.P.A. at a major firm twenty-five years before going into semi-retirement. Her limited duties at GTI amount to roughly twenty hours a week.

Executive Chef: Paul Adams, 40, received training at the Culinary Institute of Chicago and has worked some of the country's top hotels and restaurants. He wanted stability and less stress in a smaller operation and has been very happy at GTI these past five years. He is responsible for all foodservice activities and supervises cooks and dishwashers in the day shift.

Sous Chef: Kate Traylor, 22, was hired by Chef Paul four years ago to wash dishes. She began helping him with prep and soon moved into a prep-cook position. In time she discovered that cooking was her passion and entered formal training under Chef Paul two years ago. She was recently promoted to Sous Chef and is thinking about attending culinary school herself. Part of her responsibilities are to supervise cooks and dishwashers in the evening shift.

Executive Housekeeper: Olivia Lynn, 25, completed her hospitality degree and worked three years at a large hotel chain before coming to GTI. A desire to be closer to home led to her move back to the Chelsea area, that and a disdain for the corporate environment she'd previously been in. Olivia supervises the housekeeping, in-house laundry, and dry cleaning staff.

SUMMARY OF THE MODEL

1) Needs Assessment
   a. What is the problem?
   b. Who needs what?
   c. Objectives: What should the training outcomes be?

    d. Define the trainees
- Who are we training? (common profile)
- What are their learning styles?
- What do they already know?

2) Training Plan
    a. Training topics
    b. Schedule time and place
    c. Select trainers

3) Lesson Plans
    a. Behavioral objectives
    b. Select methods
    c. Content & materials
    d. Trainer directions (script & business)
    e. Trainee evaluation instruments

4) Train-the-Trainer
    a. Design formal training for trainers including:
- Adult learning principles
- Motivation & communication
- Team building & leadership
- Teaching methods
- Lesson plans

5) Implementation
    a. Preparation & practice

6) Evaluating training program
    a. Did it meet the objectives?

7) Coaching and Counseling
    a. Supervision/On-going training
    b. Recognizing and addressing personal problems

KEY WORDS

Model	Lesson Plan
Needs Assessment	Evaluation
Objectives	Coaching
Training Plan	Training Design Model

CHAPTER QUESTIONS

1. What are some models you have used in your life (such as dress pattern, model airplane, recipe, etc.)? Did you get the expected results from the model? Why or why not? Discuss the value of models.

2. Define *needs assessment,* and list the outcomes of the needs assessment.

3. Discuss the importance of needs assessment in terms of the Training Design Model's other components.

4. Describe the difference between an objective written in behavioral terms and one that is not. Why are training objectives always written in behavioral terms?

5. Write a behavioral objective for training a bus person to set a table.

6. How does training differ from education in terms of outcomes (meeting training or educational objectives)?

7. What is a *lesson plan*, and why do trainers need them?

8. What is the difference between needs assessment and evaluation? Give specific examples.

9. Define and describe coaching as opposed to authoritarian management styles. Why is coaching more effective?

10. Why do today's managers have to be able to recognize warning signs of employees' personal problems? Employees must always meet standards, but what should managers' attitudes be toward employees' personal problems?

3 *Needs Assessment Planning*

OBJECTIVES

The first step in the Training Design Model is **needs assessment**. This is where we collect appropriate data to determine the precise problem, and decide whether or not training is a feasible solution. If training is indeed the answer, our needs assessment then involves determining specific training needs. The purpose of this chapter is to describe the methods available for data collection and to explain the process for developing a needs assessment plan. This plan is essential to avoid collecting unnecessary data.

Upon completion of Chapter Three, the student should be able to

- Discuss the importance and purpose of needs assessment.
- Describe the various methods for conducting needs assessment.
- Choose appropriate methods and develop a needs assessment plan.

Planning Considerations

New operations need training programs. The task is simply to determine the scope of training and then design it. Indications of a need for training in existing operations could be such things as

1. Guest dissatisfaction, a low number of repeat guests, and/or diminishing sales.
2. Excessive turnover, absenteeism, and/or low morale.

3. High waste, low productivity, theft, disorganization, accidents.

4. Excessive damage to equipment and/or sanitation deficiencies.

Our task for existing operations is to determine whether training can alleviate any of the above problems, and, if so, proceed with its design.

There are several factors that must be considered to begin the planning process. Long-term operation goals must be addressed in terms of compatibility with the training program. If the operation has plans to change the facilities (move or expand) or the target market, the training program would also have to adapt. Would the organization be interested in spending the time and money on a program that could become obsolete? Forecasts of the labor pool, population, and the economic cycle could indicate changes that would affect an organization's training needs. The amount of time and money potentially wasted (by not considering the future) increases dramatically with the size of the operation.

Any time an organization upgrades with better equipment or procedures, training is affected, not only for employees, but for management as well. Training designers should take into account any technological advances organizations may be making in the future. It is imperative that most businesses make improvements to stay competitive.

Getting started. A survey of the facilities available for training is recommended. Also, the skill levels of current employees and management should be assessed. Neither task carries a price tag, but garners information that may be useful in avoiding assumptions that turn out incorrect and costly later. It is always better to identify limitations in advance. Management must consider training a priority and act accordingly if it is to be effective. Its support must be assured for when the time comes to implement any training program.

Types of Needs Assessments

We all have needs. Some of our needs are the same, but some are different. If I have a need for quiet and you have a need for background music, we could have a problem if we are to work together in the same room. **Individual needs** are the knowledge, skills, attitudes, and motivations a person brings to the position. Organizations can have different needs too. Some companies need risk takers and creative types, while others prefer employees who follow orders and maintain company procedures. People are not all the same, and neither are companies.

Organizational needs are determined by the company's mission, philosophy, and goals. They encompass the entire organization and could involve such things as reducing turnover, encouraging ethical behavior, or increasing productivity. If employee needs are opposed to the organization's needs, the relationship may not be satisfactory for both parties.

All positions are not alike. **Position needs** are the required behaviors for the job and are determined through **task analysis**, where we break down the particular task or duty into its separate steps. Some positions require good communication skills and the ability to deal with customers. Other positions might demand organizational ability, manual dexterity, or a certain expertise. We know it is essential to match people to positions so they are able to excel. Though some guy might be a terrific tap-dancer, his talents would be wasted cutting diamonds. A better fit might be in a winery squashing grapes. Basically, though, when organizational, position, and individual needs are all in line, the potential for success is enhanced. For the design of effective training, all three types of needs should be identified.

What we think we need and what we really need sometimes are not the same. Sometimes what companies say and what they do can be at odds. An organization may advertise for a self-starter but may really want an order-taker. Needs assessments endeavor to find out the "real" needs.

Needs Assessment Methods

There are many ways to obtain information. The method we choose is determined by whether we are an existing or new operation. We also want to consider the type of information we need to obtain. If we need information about future economic trends, we will probably not survey our wait staff. We might, however, survey the wait staff if we are trying to assess their specific needs. Through surveys or interviews with employees, we could find out what benefits are preferred (i.e. health care, child-care, tuition reimbursements). We could also find out what they expect from their jobs— things like money, friends, social opportunities, advancement, and so forth. An observation alone would not give us this type of information.

When we identify the needs of our employees, along with their particular skills and abilities, we can attempt to meet those needs within the operation in terms of career ladders and long-term employment. Training can be tailored to move the employees in directions to better match future positions.

Organizational needs can be obtained by interviewing or surveying top management. The party line, however, may be different from reality. To remedy this, we could interview and/or survey line managers and workers to see if they agree on the organization's needs. If there is disagreement, further inquiry would be necessary. Perhaps there is an owner or board of directors who might have an opinion. Top management should be made aware if there is a disagreement in this area so that modifications can be made to correct the disparity.

Assessing position needs is very similar to job analysis (the first step in the Human Resources Model described in Chapter Two). The purpose of needs assessment with respect to a specific position is to determine the duties and responsibilities of that position (like in job analysis), but to do so in greater depth. In an existing operation we can ask an employee doing the job. The employee, however, may say one thing and do another, so we can cross-check by observing the employee's actions. We will probably want to ask and observe several employees because one employee may not be doing the job correctly. If all the employees' descriptions and performances match, we could check that information against what management says the employees should be doing. Getting the same information from different sources and in different ways is called **triangulation**. If all the sources and information match, we have come, as closely as we can, to the real need.

Assessing the needs of a position in a new operation is a little more challenging. There are no employees to ask or watch who are actually doing the job. The training has to be designed, yet the new hires need to be ready for opening day. Just like in job analysis, we will look at similar operations and see what their employees are expected to do in the same positions. We can talk to management and others who have the organizational vision of the position and how it fits with others in the operation. That's assuming human resources documents are completed and correct. In new operations, job analysis and needs assessment can be combined to obtain all the data necessary for job descriptions and specifications . . . and, in addition, the data necessary to determine the needs of the position can also be found.

Employee meetings are important. Get-togethers where workers feel free to offer opinions, observations, and suggestions are another way of assessing training needs. We should never rely on just one means of assessment, but rather utilize at least two complementary methods, such as interviews and observation. Two or more sources will make our data more reliable.

Existing Documents

For existing operations, we will review documents such as job descriptions, job specifications, policy and procedure manuals, training materials, and so on. If the information is current and valid, it could save us time. We will use or modify anything that will work. Training design does not necessarily have to be original. It just has to be effective.

A company that already has a formal training program should continually assess needs, being cognizant of any changes in business or problems that arose in the past. Reviewing customer comment cards, employee performance appraisals, conducting exit interviews with employees who leave, documenting critical incidents, and observing the products (menu items, service encounter, etc.) can indicate a need for additional training or for modifying existing training.

Documents are available that list duties for a multitude of occupations. *The National Council on Vocational Education*, the *Vocational-Technical Education Consortium of States*, and *Vocational Education Services* are just three organizations that have prepared comprehensive occupational competencies and job duties. The *Dictionary of Occupational Titles* is readily available and extremely useful for developing and selecting instructional materials for training in the hospitality industry. If nothing else, the documents can serve as a reference point.

Needs Assessment Is Common Sense

Needs assessment is front-end evaluation. We are all practiced evaluators. We make decisions each day as to the appropriate clothes to wear by checking our appointment calendars so we do not show up for an important meeting in our gardening ensemble. We check the weather so that we are warm or cool enough and have the proper rain or snow gear if necessary. Every time we go to the grocery store we have to make selections from shelves of similar products. We read the label, consider the price, the amount, the quality of the product, and we choose the item that best meets our needs.

We probably do not use an evaluation checklist when we go to the grocery store, but we are, however, going through a series of questions that we answer to determine the best match. And so it is with needs assessment. We first identify what it is we need to find out. Then we ask ourselves what we need to know to find it out, and whom we can ask or what we can do to get that information. This is common sense—not really any different from deciding what we want for dinner. We feel hungry. We look at what is available to eat in the refrigerator. We imagine eating the things we find. Did they taste good in our imagination? Which item sounds most appealing? How hungry am I? Is there enough to eat? How long does it take to cook? Do I need other ingredients? Do I want to or do I have time to go to the store? Do I have any money? We may even do a quick nutritional analysis in our head before making a dinner decision.

In needs assessment we are going to systematize what we do automatically in our daily lives. We have a list of methods for collecting data and will select the methods best suited to the type of data we need to collect. We will also consider the logistics of collecting data (time for interviews, survey development, etc.) and how we will analyze the data once it is collected. If we conduct open-ended interviews or group meetings, or ask employees to fill out questionnaires, what will we do with all that information? Do we have a way of putting it together that makes sense? We might decide it would be better to ask specific questions and have a form for classifying answers.

Employee Input in Needs Assessment

Our approach to needs assessment can determine the ultimate success of any training program. We must consider the feelings of everyone involved. We will want everyone to enthusiastically embrace the new training program if it is an existing operation. Many people do not like change and may resist.

We should attempt to involve the line staff in the needs assessment process, explaining purpose and intent, while reassuring employees that we are not evaluating their work, but, rather, need their help to design new or improved training for future employees. Needs assessment can be threatening to employees if they do not have a complete understanding of the purpose and the process. Employees' input is essential because they are the people actually doing the jobs, and their knowledge is reality-based.

Needs assessment at best is ongoing. Management should be continuously aware of changes in organizational, position, and individual needs. Unless we have a formal means of assessing, we can miss important information or changes. Line supervisors should be consulted frequently as they see the results of training, and their feedback can be used as the basis for improvements. We must be open to and able to modify our training programs. Ownership of the training design process and the final program must be shared with the entire organization.

Summary of Considerations and Methods

The needs assessment process begins with reviewing everything that already exists. Things like facilities, the staff, documents, financial and top management support for training. We forecast changes that could occur and affect training. Taking the present and future into consideration, we then must find out the organization, individual, and position needs. We ask, "What do we need to know, and how can we obtain this information?"

We spend most of our design effort on position needs. However, if we ignore individual and organization needs and present and future realities/possibilities, we could end up with a training program that is already out of date and too deficient to modify.

The data collected in the needs assessment process must be used as the basis for the training design. It is in needs assessment that we collect all information required for the remaining six steps in the training design model. If we keep the model in mind during the needs assessment planning process, we'll know better which questions to ask to obtain information needed for the remaining steps.

Step #1	#2	#3	#4	#5	#6	#7
Needs Assessment	Training Plan	Lesson Plans	Trainer Training	Training Implementation	Training Evaluation	Coaching & Counseling

Planning Checklist

Facilities:

• What space and provisions are available for training?

Management support:

• Will top management provide time, money, and authority? (This will determine whether we can successfully implement the training program.)

- How much money will be available? (This can determine the scope of the training.)

Forecasts of labor pool, economic cycle, and population:

- Will the makeup of available labor change so that our training becomes inadequate later on?
- Will there be enough employees in the future?
- Will fluctuating economic times affect our workforce or business?
- Will we have more or less or the same number of people available as customers and/or workers?

Technology/equipment upgrades:

- Are improvements or changes foreseen that could affect training?

Expected changes in facilities or target market:

- In the future, is the organization planning on moving or expanding?
- Is the organization planning on targeting new markets that could require different training?

Organizational needs:

- What is the organization's mission and philosophy?
- What results does top management expect from the training program?
- What does top management expect the training to look like? (style, scope, etc.)
- Which positions will be included in the training program?
- What problems does top management believe the training program can correct?
- Are the problems real, and can the training program correct them?

Individual needs:

- What are the skill levels, attitudes, and knowledge of current and potential workers?
- What do workers expect from their jobs?
- What particular needs (child-care, health care, vacations, tuition reimbursement, flexible hours, etc.) do workers have that can impact job performance?

Position needs:

- Obtain a copy of the organizational chart.
- What are the duties and responsibilities of each position? (Job descriptions)
- What are the qualifications necessary to do each of the positions? (Job specifications)
- What type of training is necessary for each position?
- Task Analysis

Data Collection Methods:

- Surveys
- Interviews
- Observations
- Employee meetings/discussions
- Existing documents
- Dictionary of Occupational Titles, etc.
- Customer comment cards/customer input
- Employee exit interviews
- Employee performance appraisals
- Critical incidents reports
- Inspections of products

Develop Data Collection Instruments

Develop surveys, interview questions, and observation checklists, considering how the data will be analyzed.

Prepare materials to explain the purpose of needs assessment—to reassure employees and obtain their involvement in the process.

Collect and analyze data.

When step one of the model is completed, we will have enough information to develop the training plan.

Case Study—The Garden Terrace Inn

Planning the Needs Assessment

Jim Charles, General Manager, contracted with our Hospitality Training Design firm to provide training for all line positions at The Garden Terrace Inn (GTI). We will use the planning checklist to prepare for our first site visit. The sources of information are the general manager, department managers, workers, existing documents, and outside sources. We reorganize items on the planning checklist into source groups and determine the best method for obtaining information. We may wish to ask the same questions of two or more sources, and we may wish to use two or more methods to obtain this information. [Justifications for the choice will be in brackets.]

Organizational needs—Questions for the general manager (GM):

1. What space and provisions are available for training? (Also observe.)
2. Will top management provide time, money, and authority?
3. How much money will be available?
4. Are improvements in technology or equipment foreseen?
5. Is GTI planning on moving or expanding in the future?
6. Is GTI planning on targeting new markets in the future?
7. What results does top management expect from the training program?
8. What does top management expect the training to look like?
9. How should we introduce the needs assessment process to the staff and get their involvement?
10. Which positions are to be included in the training program?
11. What problems does top management believe the training program can correct? (We will need to determine whether the problems are real and, if so, whether training can alleviate the problems.)
12. What is the mission and philosophy of GTI?

Method: Interview

    (This is a smaller operation, so interviews are easy to conduct. If we were conducting needs assessment for a national hotel chain, we might choose to develop a survey that could be sent to all department heads or managers.)

Individual needs—Questions for department heads and workers:

1. What are the skill levels, attitudes, and knowledge of workers?
2. What do workers expect from their jobs?
3. What particular needs (child care, health care, vacations, tuition reimbursement, flexible hours, etc.) do workers have that can impact job performances?

Method: Survey to all workers and department heads. Follow-up interview with department heads.

Position needs

- Organization chart
- Job descriptions
- Job specifications
- What type of training is necessary for each of the positions?
- Are there any pertinent human resource and/or training documents available?
- Task Analysis

Method: Request documents from general manager in advance of site visit.

- Interview department heads and selected workers.
- Observe selected workers.

    (Comparing any existing documents, interviews with workers and department heads, plus observations of workers will verify the validity of the documents or provide information to modify the documents or construct documents if necessary.)

    (Task analysis, where we further break down each task in each position into step-by-step directions, will be addressed in Chapter Four.)

Other needs: Forecasts of labor pool, economic cycle, and population

- Will the make-up of available labor change?
- Will there be enough employees later on?
- Will good or bad economic times affect GTI's workforce or business?
- Will GTI have more, less, or the same number of people available as customers?

Method: Demographic statistics, research articles, labor and economic forecasts.

Planning the Data Collection

We know the information we need to obtain and have decided on the best methods for collection. Now we must devise a plan for assembling data. The following is a list of things we need to do:

1. Request existing documents (see plan above and send letter).
2. Assemble general manager questions for interview (see plan above).
3. Make an appointment and interview GM.
4. Collect and analyze population, labor, and economic forecasts.
5. Develop questionnaire for staff and department heads.
6. Prepare materials (script) to present the needs assessment process to employees.
7. Plan and implement task analysis.

The first three items on the list are simple and can be done right away. Questions for the GM were determined from the planning checklist. Information from that interview will be used later in items six and seven. Most information in item four can be found on the Internet. Items five, six, and seven will be addressed in Chapter Four.

SUMMARY

Needs assessment is the step most often forgotten, yet it might be most important in the model. It is time-consuming and expensive to design training. Without needs assessment we could be designing training that does not solve the problem (and is subsequently a waste of resources). We want to make sure our training is necessary and effective. The needs assessment planning checklist helps us to approach any training challenge with a model process. By using common sense, we can determine whether we need additional information for a particular situation and fit it into the checklist.

KEY WORDS

Needs Assessment	Triangulation
Individual Needs	Position Needs
Organizational Needs	Task Analysis

CHAPTER THOUGHT QUESTIONS

1. Think about a time when you were being interviewed for a position you really wanted. How did you decide what to wear, what to bring with you, how to prepare for the interview, and how to answer questions? Please detail in writing your preparation for the job interview. How does it compare to the needs assessment process described in Chapter Three?

2. Has there ever been a time when you did not adequately prepare for an interview or some other important situation? What was the result of lack of preparation, and what could you have done differently? (If for either of these questions you lacked the experience you were asked to describe, then make up one that allows you the opportunity to explain the importance and consequences of adequate preparation.)

3. If your boss told you to put together a proposal for an employee benefit package, identify the information you would need, from whom, and describe the methods you would utilize to get that information.

4. Thinking about a current or previous job, list your individual needs at the time in that particular job, list the position needs for the position you held, and list the organization needs for the company you worked for. Focus your attention on the various needs as described in Chapter Three.

5. List factors in existing operations that are indications of training needs. In a current or previous job, discuss and describe any indications of training needs you have noticed and suggest training topics that might alleviate the training need.

6. Define the concept of triangulation and describe how it relates to needs assessment. Describe a situation in your personal life where triangulation helped you make a good decision.

7. Why is it important for employees to be involved in the needs assessment process? How do you get their honest input? What would keep employees from being honest?

8. To open a new operation, the need for training is obvious. Needs assessment is necessary to make sure the training we design is necessary and effective. How do we do needs assessment when there aren't any existing employees, management, or customers? Be specific, please.

9. Discuss why the Needs Assessment Planning Checklist is useful. Is it a model? Why/why not?

10. List the various data collection instruments. Describe pros and cons of each method, and discuss the importance of considering data analysis before collecting the data.

4 Implementing Needs Assessment

OBJECTIVES

We have devised the needs assessment plan. What we need now is to find out from whom the information will be gathered, and how this will be accomplished. In Chapter Three we put together the following "to do" list.

1. Request existing documents (see plan and send letter).

2. Assemble general manager questions for interview.

3. Make an appointment and interview GM.

4. Collect and analyze the population, labor, and economic forecasts.

5. Develop the questionnaire for staff and department heads.

6. Prepare materials (script) to present the needs assessment process to employees.

7. Plan and implement task analysis.

We must now develop appropriate instruments for items two, five, six, and seven in order to implement the plan.

Developing reliable and valid instruments is a skill that can be taught. The purpose of this chapter is to present questionnaire and interview construction instruction that will enable us to devise effective questionnaires and interview schedules that will result in the collection of necessary data. This chapter will also address developing scripts for introducing the needs assessment process to existing staff. Task analysis, where we break down each duty on the job into sequential steps, is the basis of training design and will be dealt with in Chapter Five.

Upon completion of Chapter Four, the student should be able to

- Develop interview schedules to obtain appropriate data for any particular purpose.

- Develop a reliable and valid questionnaire to obtain appropriate data for any particular purpose.

- Devise a plan and script for introducing the needs assessment process to staff in an already-existing operation.

Interviews and Questionnaires

The purpose of both interviews and questionnaires is to obtain information from people. Whether we choose a questionnaire or an interview format has to do with the type of information we wish to obtain and the number of people involved.

Interviews

An **interview** is a face-to-face verbal question-and-answer interaction between interviewer and respondent. When we want to find out specific information, we will devise a **structured** list of questions. If we conduct interviews with several people for the same information, we can use the same list of questions and compare and contrast answers later. We generally choose the interview format when we are interested in gathering information from only a few people. Interviews are time-consuming, thus expensive to use.

Interviews may be **unstructured**—that is, without a specific list of questions. An unstructured interview is useful when we are not sure what information we are looking for. While we will generally use structured interviews in needs assessment, we should be open to any other information that may come to us in the interview. One of the benefits of the interview method is that people will often say more in person than they would in writing. Also, their body language and tone of voice may give us important information that we could never have obtained on a questionnaire. In interviews we often allow respondents the opportunity to expand on their answers by asking **open questions**. Open questions do not give specific answer options. They are instead phrased to elicit more and less controlled information.

Closed: Do you like to read?   ☐ Yes   ☐ No

Open: What kinds of things do you like to read? If you do not like to read, why not?

It would be easy to count the number of people who answered yes and no in the above closed example and then say, "X number like to read," and, "Y number do not like to read." If we were interested in finding out if people liked or did not like to read, this would be the easiest and most effective way to find out. If, however, we were interested in their reading habits and motivations, the closed question would not be useful. We can get more information from open questions, but they will be more difficult to tabulate because there could be as many answers as there are respondents.

The Garden Terrace Inn—Interview Development

Our GM interview will be conducted utilizing a written list of questions to avoid wasting time with questions that are unnecessary or fail to elicit specific responses. We may add additional questions during the interview if pertinent to the original need we are attempting to assess. We note the answers to our questions in the interview in writing and do not rely on memory. We may find that a question we ask is not clear to the respondent. Because interviews are face-to-face, though, we can clarify the question immediately.

We used the needs assessment planning checklist in Chapter Three to put together a list of questions to ask the general manager in an interview. Organizational needs must be identified first because they determine the scope and direction of training. We will simply reorganize and clarify questions and rewrite them on a separate piece of paper with room for the GM's answers.

Organizational needs—Questions for the general manager:

1. What is the mission and philosophy of GTI?

2. What problems do you believe the training program can correct? (We will need to determine if the problems are real and, if so, whether training can alleviate them.)

3. What results do you expect from the training program?

4. What do you expect the training to look like?

5. Which positions are to be included in the training program?

6. How much time and authority will you provide?

7. How much money will be available?

8. What space and provisions are available for training? (Also observe.)

9. Are improvements in technology or equipment foreseen?

10. Is GTI planning on moving or expanding in the future?

11. Is GTI planning on targeting new markets in the future?

    (If respondent answered "yes" to any of the last three questions, we need to ask how we will handle changes in terms of updating the training, etc.)

12. How should we introduce the needs assessment process to the staff and get their involvement?

So, we have a structured list of questions for the GM. They are open questions, and we will ask them in a conversational form and follow up with more probing/clarification questions and further statements to establish understanding and rapport.

Questionnaires

A **questionnaire** is a written form containing questions and answer options that is administered either verbally (like in a phone survey you may have experienced), or in writing (like surveys you may have received in the mail and been asked to fill in and return). Surveys generally ask **closed questions** where answer options are specified such as, "male/female," "yes/no," or "Strongly agree/agree/undecided/disagree/strongly disagree." Questionnaires are usually used when data is to be collected from a large group of people. They are relatively easy to analyze, although time consuming to construct properly.

Questionnaires must be **pilot tested** to be sure they work before administering them to the selected respondents. A pilot test is where we administer the questionnaire to just a few people who resemble the people the questionnaire was designed for. We do this to see if they have any trouble understanding questions or how to answer them. In the past, we may have been asked to fill out a questionnaire and found some of the questions to be unanswerable. Perhaps there wasn't a response that was a good match for our opinion, or the question brought up conditions in our mind that were not addressed in the available responses, or the question may have been contradictory.

The pilot test allows us to test construction of the questionnaire so we can make any necessary corrections before we give it to our target group. It is a waste of resources to administer a questionnaire that people return with question marks and blank spots. Poorly constructed questionnaires can frustrate people and result in nonresponses.

The pilot test also allows us to tabulate and analyze the results to see if there are any problems that need to be corrected before the real questionnaire is administered. We may find that we need an additional question for clarification, or the numbering system is inadequate, or anything else that gets in the way of efficient analysis. Even the most experienced designers need to pilot test. It's like proofreading our own papers—we often do not catch our own mistakes, and what seemed perfectly clear to us may be incomprehensible to someone else.

Questionnaire Development Checklist

The following is a list of things to consider when constructing a questionnaire. It is a good idea to check our questionnaire against the list and address discrepancies before conducting the pilot test.

1. The questionnaire should be easy to read and well organized. It should not be crowded or busy. The questions should be simply stated, and easy to figure out.

2. The questionnaire should not be too long or take too much time to fill out. Be sure it is no longer than necessary.

3. Questions should not sound threatening to the respondent.

4. No unnecessary questions should be asked. Consider how each relates to a particular research topic.

5. Be sure to ask for just one answer per question. For instance, "I believe that the administration is always right and people who miss more than three days a month should be terminated. ☐ Yes ☐ No" This actually asks two questions. A respondent could believe the administration is right, yet not think a person should be terminated, or the other way around. Only if the respondent agreed or disagreed with both questions could he or she comfortably answer yes or no.

6. Don't ask a question based on an assumption that may be incorrect, such as "Employees who use the Internet at work for personal business should be ☐ terminated ☐ disciplined ☐ demoted." This assumes that employees consider the act as wrong. If they do not feel that using the Internet for personal business at work is wrong, they cannot answer the question.

7. Ask questions so that they flow sequentially, if possible. The sequence of questions should make sense to the respondent.

8. Can the answers be easily tabulated and analyzed?

9. Has the questionnaire been pilot tested and corrected if necessary?

The Garden Terrace Inn—Questionnaire

We will now develop a survey instrument to be administered to all department heads and workers to determine their individual needs. We chose the questionnaire format because we have to survey many people. We would not bother constructing a survey instrument for just a few people. To facilitate this, we provide boxes for them to check rather than have them write long explanations and comments that might or might not answer the questions and would be difficult to tabulate and analyze.

Questionnaires must be kept simple and to the point. Data collected in such a way is easily analyzed.

Our research questions are

1. What are the skill levels, attitudes, and knowledge of workers?

2. What do workers expect from their jobs?

3. What particular needs do workers have (i.e. child care, health care, vacations, tuition reimbursement, flexible hours, etc.) that can impact their performances?

The questions will be posed to determine individual needs. We are trying to identify our staff—who they are, and what is important to them. We will be designing training for them or employees similar to them, and it must be a good fit.

Employees will have been introduced to the needs assessment process prior to filling out the questionnaire and should have been reassured as to its nonevaluative nature. However, we still must be cognizant of how employees may interpret our questions and make ourselves available for further clarification and/or reassurance.

The individual needs portion of needs assessment may be the smallest. Position needs is by far the largest. As a result, our instrument does not have to be very big. We have asked just ten questions starting with the employee's name. This is not scientific research, and we do not have to protect the anonymity of the sample respondents. We are interested in who has what to say. Later, we may want to talk to the individual who filled out a particular questionnaire for further information or clarification. This is a small operation, and because we are not dealing with thousands of employees, we can afford the time for some individual interaction if it is useful.

An employee's actual position in the company would be pertinent information. We might find that all dishwashers or servers have the same needs and that they differ from housekeeper's needs. We will be able to consider their levels of education, which makes a difference in the way we design and present training.

Unless management intends to change its recruiting procedures, it is likely that any new employees will be similar to the present employees. Thus, by identifying education levels, needs, expectations, and time on the job for current employees, we can identify a profile of the typical employee for each position. We will then use this to develop training specific to each position that should be a good match for future trainees.

The Garden Terrace Inn Employee Questionnaire

1. Name: _____

2. What is your position?
   - ☐ Cook
   - ☐ Dishwasher
   - ☐ Housekeeper
   - ☐ Front Desk
   - ☐ Night Auditor
   - ☐ Server

   Other: _____

3. How long have you worked at GTI?
   - ☐ Three months or less
   - ☐ Between four months and one year

    ☐ Between one year and two years

    ☐ Between two years and three years

    ☐ Over three years

4. What education have you obtained?

    ☐ Have not yet completed high school

    ☐ High school diploma

    ☐ Vocational-Technical school certificate/degree

        Subject: _____

    ☐ Some college

        Major: _____

    ☐ College degree

        Major: _____

        Other: _____

5. After you have checked any of the items below that you would like to be able to obtain from your job, please number them in terms of importance to you with the number one being the most important.

                                                              Rank

    ☐ Money   _____

    ☐ Friends and social life   _____

    ☐ Job security   _____

    ☐ Promotion   _____

    ☐ Personal growth   _____

    ☐ Challenge   _____

    ☐ Professional growth   _____

    ☐ Independence (not a lot of supervision)   _____

    ☐ Structure and supervision   _____

        Other: _____   _____

                     _____   _____

                     _____   _____

                     _____   _____

6. Please check any of the following needs you may have, and then number them in terms of importance to you.

Rank

☐ Vacation   _____

☐ Tuition reimbursement   _____

☐ Full-time hours   _____

☐ Cross training and job rotation   _____

☐ Inn discounts for self and family   _____

☐ Employee parties or activities   _____

☐ Employee wellness program   _____

Other: _____   _____

    _____   _____

    _____   _____

    _____   _____

7. In your current position, which would you prefer?

☐ More responsibility

☐ Less responsibility

☐ I am satisfied with the present level of responsibility.

8. In your current position, which would you prefer?

☐ More supervision

☐ Less supervision

☐ I am satisfied with the present level of supervision.

9. I might like the additional responsibility of training new employees.

☐ Yes

☐ No

10. Please write in the space below any comments or suggestions that you think could help us to better know and meet your needs.

We would then, of course, pilot the questionnaire with several people similar to the employees to make sure they understand it, that the questions make sense, and that answers can be tabulated and analyzed with ease. We will also want to ascertain whether or not the information collected is useful. It's easier and less costly to modify the questionnaire before administering it to everyone.

Prepare Employees for Needs Assessment

Employee involvement in needs assessment is essential within existing operations. Needs assessment can look and feel very much like employee appraisal. We are, however, not interested in evaluating employees' performance, but rather in finding out what they actually do and think about what they do. We want their input. If they think their responses to our questions will in any way hurt them, they may not give us useful, honest answers. They may say what they think we want to hear, or what they think they should say, rather than the truth. They must be reassured that their answers will be used to develop training for future employees and will not in any way credit or discredit their own performance.

Depending on the operation, we might choose to hold an employee meeting or several shift meetings to explain the process and purpose. The whole point is to reassure employees and make them comfortable and open to involvement in the process. How we accomplish that will differ from operation to operation. We must assess the climate and determine what approach will be most effective. Management will usually know what works best with their particular employees, and we can also pay attention to our surroundings. With practice we can tune into what people respond to.

The Garden Terrace Inn Introduction to Needs Assessment

After interviewing the GM, we decided to hold a 45-minute paid employee meeting to present the needs assessment process and purpose. There will be another meeting for those who could not attend the first. The employees know and trust Jim, the GM, and it was determined that he would enthusiastically introduce us and the plan. We then described exactly what we will be doing and what we need the employees to do, and why we are doing it. The following is the script we will loosely follow in the meeting.

> **Jim:** "Good afternoon, everyone! It is nice to all be in the same place at the same time for a change. We have come a long way in the past six years, and it's all because of you and your professionalism and dedication to gracious service. I am proud to be a part of The Garden Terrace Inn, and I am very proud of all of you.

"As we have grown and established our reputation, we are now at a point where it makes sense to formalize our training program. We have never really had one. We have tried to make sure that new employees knew what they were doing before working with our guests, but there was never a specific plan. Many of you have taken new employees under your wing and shown them what to do, but you were not given the time and materials that would have made it easier.

"All of us are too busy to devise formal training, so I have brought in Hospitality Training Design to put together a program for us that will result in consistent training. This will be easier for us to do than what we have been doing. No outsider can tell us how to do our jobs, of course, so it is essential that we get involved in this process and clue them in on what we do and what we need . . . so they can design training that really works for us. I want you to make them feel welcome and give them your complete cooperation."

Designer: "Hello, everyone! I am so happy to be here. I know why Jim is so proud of The Garden Terrace Inn and all of you. I was here three years ago at the most beautiful wedding I have ever attended. The food was wonderful, the service was unobtrusive and gracious, and the ambiance was perfect. We are not changing anything you do. What we are doing is putting together a written training program which will help GTI train new employees to do just what you already do.

"We will be around for the next few days, observing, asking questions, and getting your input. We will *not* be evaluating your performance. You know how to do your jobs. You know how the positions at GTI fit together to result in the total care your guests receive. You know the things that new employees need to know and do. We are going to combine your job expertise with our training design expertise . . . and work with you to develop the most efficient, effective training program possible.

"None of your input will be used against you in any way . . . or manipulated to judge your performance. If you are aware of any improvements that could be made, or have any suggestions at all, please be sure to share them with us. We will begin with assessing needs—the needs of the inn, the needs of the positions, and your needs. You will all be receiving a questionnaire that we would appreciate your filling out and returning to us. We will be asking some of you questions about what you do and your thoughts about the job. We will also be observing selected employees—not to evaluate your performance—but to see if what you are actually doing matches what you say you do. In that way, we will not miss anything that should be in the training.

"The training you have been giving new employees has worked, and some of you might think designing a formal training program is a waste of time and money. But it is not. Well-designed formal training programs work better and easier and faster. They take no thought. All the thought has already been done and written down. Some of you who are interested may want to become 'official' trainers. You will be given paid release time and training to train new employees. If any of you have ever experienced formal training, you know that it works much better. So, please share your job knowledge with us and help us to make the best training program we can.

"Are there any questions?"

CONCLUSION

Needs assessment is common sense with a few technical skills thrown in. By using a needs assessment planning checklist, we can determine what we need to find out and from whom and how. Instruments are developed to obtain the specific information in a style that matches the people we are trying to ask. We are simply asking ourselves, "What do I want to know, and how can I find it out?"

KEY WORDS

Interview	Unstructured Interviews
Open Questions	Questionnaire
Closed Questions	Pilot test
Structured Interviews	

CHAPTER THOUGHT QUESTIONS

1. Think about a previous job interview you have experienced. Did the interviewer have a list of questions to ask you? Did the interviewer write down your answers? Who did most of the

talking? You, or the interviewer? Were you asked job-specific questions? What was the objective for the interview? Do you think that objective was met? Why or why not?

2. Describe advantages and disadvantages of the interview format. For what types of situations might an interview be the best way to obtain the desired information?

3. Define and describe the difference between structured and unstructured interviews. What are the advantages and disadvantages of both structured and unstructured interviews? Give examples of situations where each type might be the better choice.

4. Define and describe the difference between open and closed questions. What are the advantages and disadvantages of both open and closed questions, and when might each be a better choice?

5. Think of any surveys you have been requested to fill out recently. Were there any questions where none of the answer choices matched your response? Were there any questions that were not clear to you? What characteristics of surveys (you have participated in) have you found annoying?

6. Define and describe pilot testing. What is the purpose of pilot testing, and why is it necessary?

7. What are the advantages and disadvantages of the survey data collection method? When is it best to use a survey rather than another data collection method?

8. How are surveys and interviews tabulated? How do you handle and what do you do with the information you obtain from the survey or interview?

9. Discuss the purpose of needs assessment and why it is essential for employees in existing operations to be involved. Describe how management might go about preparing employees for this involvement, and the pitfalls management would want to avoid by adequately preparing employees.

10. Discuss how needs assessment is a matter of common sense and how questionnaires and interviews relate to it.

5 Planning Job Analysis

OBJECTIVES

We have determined organizational and individual needs. We have requested any existing documents (such as job descriptions) that will begin to identify position needs. In Chapter Five we will construct the instruments needed to identify the needs of each position. We will then develop a plan for analyzing each job, breaking it into sequential steps to assist us in the design of effective training. Through the **job analysis** process, we will also be looking at job design to enable us to modify the way jobs are done with an eye toward making them more efficient and effective.

Upon completion of Chapter Five, the student should be able to

- Describe the instructional design process.
- Describe the relationship between jobs, duties, and tasks.
- Describe how to develop a job list and how this list differs from a job description.
- Define task analysis and explain why it is important.
- Discuss work simplification and motion economy and how and why we utilize the principles in job design.

Instructional Design

Instructional design is the systematic development of materials and methods for teaching a specific body of knowledge. **Training design** is instructional design aimed at teaching a person to do a specific job. Perhaps the best way to come to an understanding of instructional design is through examples. Have you ever taken a quiz and not finished all the questions because you had not been aware that there were additional questions on the backside of the paper? Have you ever handed in an exam and forgotten to put your name on it? These are examples of some of the little steps we want to remember to include in our instruction—steps that explain how to do the task or duty. They may not actually be part of the duty, but, if left out, may make its completion impossible. Adding a line for "Name" to an exam reminds students to put their name on the exam. "Continued," or, "more on the back," or, "turn page," all alert students to the fact that there are more questions to be answered. A poor grade because of a test-taking mistake rather than a knowledge mistake can and should be avoided by instructional designers.

Have you ever tried to follow directions to someone's house and found there was a street or a turn missing? Once we know how to get to the person's house, it is easy. But initially, without that step-by-step instruction, locating a person's house might involve driving around in circles till eventually stumbling upon the place only by accident. Avoiding such confusion is the idea behind instructional design. We make sure all the steps are there in the right order, that they are the right steps, and the directions for following the steps are complete and correct. We never assume that someone knows a step that is obvious to us. Every unnecessary assumption is a mistake waiting to happen.

Training design takes into consideration the organizational and individual needs but focuses on position needs. The steps at this point are to

1. Identify all the duties for each position.
2. Break down each duty into sequential steps.
3. Identify performance standards for each duty and step.

Job Lists

A **job list** identifies all the duties for a specific position. A server has a different job list than a cook because they have different duties. A **duty** is one specific task an employee does that is part of the total job. One duty of a server might be to fill the salt and pepper shakers, while one duty of a housekeeper could be to make the beds.

A good starting point for assembling a job list is a job description. A job description is a human resources management tool that lists all the main duties an employee does in a particular position. It describes the job. A job list is a list of *all* the duties of the position, so it is similar but much more complete. In start-up operations, it would make sense to obtain all the detailed information necessary for job lists and training design while doing the initial job analysis. In existing operations, however, we can begin with the job description and (using the same tools as for job analysis) then delve deeper into the job to result in a complete list of all duties performed in the particular position.

When we think about a server job, the main duties are usually taking and serving drink and food orders. A server, though, might do many other things as well, such as stock the wait station, make coffee, bus tables, set tables, prepare salads, fill salt and pepper shakers, dust the dining room, rearrange tables, clean chairs, seat guests, and/or do various cleaning side-work tasks. We have to find out exactly what servers actually do (or should be doing) in order to design training that instructs new servers how to do the job as prescribed by the organization.

In an existing operation we can ask the servers what they do—have them list all their duties. It is possible they could forget something or say something that they do not really do, so we want to cross-check by watching them do the job. That way we can compare what they say they do with what they actually do, and then see if there are any differences. We might want to watch a couple of different servers to see if they both do and say the same thing. We can also ask them if there are additional duties they think they should be doing or that they are doing that they do not think they should be doing. Finally, we can ask managers and/or supervisors for their opinions.

If all the information we collect is the same from all sources, we have an accurate job list. If there are variations, though, we must figure out what should be on the job list. We can do this by perhaps holding a meeting with servers and management. Together we can work out a reasonable and accurate job list. This is possible so long as the servers understand they are not being evaluated (and do not in any way feel threatened).

At the same time we should ask servers about training needs—i.e., what they have experienced and what they think new servers need in terms of training. Our employees often have a better grasp of training needs because they have to work with new employees, and it is in their best interest to have new employees who are well trained.

The job list is a list of all duties that make up the job or position. Once we have the job list, the next step is *task analysis*, or the breakdown of job duties into sequential steps. A **task** is one step in a duty. Task analysis is not difficult. It is tedious! Not everyone has the patience to do complete task analysis, but mistakes made from incomplete task analysis can be costly and frustrating later on. The findings from task analysis become the actual instruction that we incorporate into lesson plans for the training sessions.

Let us say that one duty on a server job list is setting tables. In order to train someone to set a table, we need to know how it is done and what the outcome should be (performance standard). We will break down the duty into sequential steps. This is task analysis. We can ask the servers, "What do you do first?"

The steps could be

1. Go to the wait station and get napkins, silverware, and bread and butter plates. [Then ask: How many place settings? Which pieces of silverware? How do you carry them to the table? Do you use a tray?]

2. Fold the napkins and place them on the table. [Then ask: How do you fold the napkins? Where and how are the napkins placed at each place setting?]

3. Place the silverware and bread and butter plates at each place. [Then ask: Where are they placed?]

4. Arrange the centerpiece and/or candle and salt and pepper shakers in the center of the table. [Then ask: How are they arranged? What should the set table look like? How long should it take to set the table?]

We need a job list, task analysis, and training information for each of the positions we are going to design training for. Part of task analysis is the **performance standard**, or, precisely how the duty should be performed and/or what it should look like when completed. The performance standard for setting the table could be in the form of a diagram of what the set table should look like. In the server example, we can either obtain all the information at one time or interview them several times for different purposes. Interviews of this nature could be rather time consuming. Time will have to be allotted for interviews, and it should not interfere with the employees' work.

If there are no apparent problems with the way employees currently are performing their jobs, we may choose to collect all the information at one interview. For new operations or operations with needs that include redesign of positions, we would first need to establish an accurate job list and then ascertain how each duty should be performed. No matter which way we decide to analyze each position, though, we must prepare a plan (ordered questions we will ask to result in desired outcomes).

Work Simplification and Motion Economy

If there is an indication that changes in job design might be necessary, we must determine what the changes should be before training is designed. **Work simplification** is the study of duties and tasks to determine the most efficient methods of performance. We analyze duties and tasks to reduce work time and eliminate unnecessary aspects of the task. Activities may also be analyzed to improve product quality, and to help develop more skill in performing the task, so that the activity may be made more pleasurable (thus, reducing stress).

When designing jobs for a new operation, management might hire a consultant to do complex formal motion studies. We, however, can use an informal method to analyze the duties and tasks. Motion study, regardless of the method, has the overall objective of developing motion-mindedness in those who work. All approaches are based on principles of body **motion economy** and body mechanics and aim either to develop better motions or to eliminate motions.

If methods and procedures have not been periodically reviewed (to determine if they are still efficient and necessary), we might want to incorporate work simplification and motion economy analysis into our job analysis process.

The steps in work simplification include

1. Select the duty.
2. Break down the duty into all the steps or tasks.
3. Question each portion of the task (what, why, how, when, where, by whom).
4. If possible, devise a better method for doing it.
5. Apply the new method.

When determining a better method, it is useful to recognize the three major areas that can be changed: the product, the work environment, and the worker. Changes in the product may result either from the use of different raw materials (frozen vegetables instead of fresh), or by using the same ingredients but changing the product (like making a large casserole instead of individual ones), or by changes in both raw ingredients and finished product (making a large casserole with frozen vegetables).

Changes in work environment might include the basic rearrangement of large kitchen equipment, new cabinets, a working surface of the proper height, organizing storage space, and so on.

Principles related to effective storage areas are

1. Place all materials and equipment used in a single type of process in the general area in which the process is carried on.
2. Store equipment and supplies at the place of first use.
3. Duplicate inexpensive equipment needed in more than one area.
4. Store items so they are easy to see, reach, and grasp.
5. Determine the worker's limits of reach.
6. Keep storage areas flexible for adaptation to changing needs.

Changes in the worker involve body positions and motions. Feelings of comfort and/or discomfort result from the repetitive use of certain muscles and strain on the worker's internal framework. Good posture—keeping the body parts in alignment—results in stability when various body weights are correctly positioned, each centered over the base of support. In correct posture, whether standing, sitting, or using a tool, muscles designed for certain uses are able to perform without injury. In incorrect posture, muscles are not aligned and strain occurs. When any part of the body gets out of line, muscular effort is required to maintain body balance in addition to whatever work the body is doing. Permanent injury may also result.

Body mechanics may be defined as the science dealing with body forces and motions. Among its major principles are

1. Using muscles effectively.
2. Using good posture.
3. Taking advantage of momentum.

Changes in activities of the body involve changes in hand and body motions. The sequence of steps in the duty may be changed. A change in motion might be putting away dishes with two hands instead of one, elimination of useless dabbing with the spoon when serving, using rhythmic motions in sweeping, any improvements in body mechanics (posture, etc.), pushing cut food from the cutting board into a bowl instead of scooping it into the hands and lifting into the bowl, and so forth.

The sequence of steps in a task may need to be ordered differently, or combined, or even eliminated. The routing of steps may be changed. For effective routing, the logical direction of the sequence of steps from beginning until completion of a task must be discovered. The goal is reduction in total distance and number of needless repetitions. Each step of a duty is to be performed with the next one in mind. For example, routing in hand dishwashing requires that stacking be done in such a place and manner as to anticipate ease in washing, drying, and storage of dishes.

Fitting steps closely together, known as **dovetailing**, may be illustrated by setting the table for the next meal (after dishwashing) without putting washed dishes away from the preceding meal. By preparing several baked products in succession, mixing bowls and utensils can be utilized more than once simply by rinsing without drying and putting away between usages. A change in the order of steps may shorten the pathway. Completing the making of a bed from one side before going to the other side is also an example.

Principles of Work Simplification

Incorporating motion economy and work simplification principles can help us to develop better and more efficient ways for employees to perform their jobs. Because the hospitality industry can be so labor intensive, it is important to analyze jobs periodically to make sure they are being done in the best ways possible. Employees may be performing duties and utilizing methods out of habit rather than need or efficiency.

The principles of work simplification are

1. Make rhythmic and smooth motions.
2. Make both hands productive at the same time.
3. Make hand and body motions few, short, and simple.
4. Maintain comfortable conditions and positions.
5. Locate material for efficiency.
6. Use the best available equipment.
7. Store materials in an orderly manner.

To determine a better method,

1. Eliminate duties or tasks.
2. Combine steps.
3. Rearrange steps, and/or simplify duties or tasks.

The Garden Terrace Inn— Job Analysis Plan

Job analysis in training design is utilizing research methods for obtaining information to result in job lists, task analysis of job list duties, performance standards, and training needs. The initial interview with the general manager (GM) (conducted to determine organizational needs) indicated that training was to be designed for the line positions of cook, dishwasher, housekeeper, front desk, night auditor, and server.

We requested existing relevant documents for all positions from the GM and department heads and subsequently received job descriptions, some policy and procedure manuals, and a few training materials. The research methods we will use to analyze the six positions will be analysis of existing documents, interviews, and observations. We will begin with the position of cook.

From the employee questionnaire we found that all six cooks were high school graduates with little or no formal training or education after high school. Most had worked at GTI between one and three years. Their prime motivations were money and job security. They were satisfied with the level of responsibility and supervision, and two indicated an interest in becoming trainers.

The following is the job description for the position of cook. Chef Paul told us that he has written recipes but that the training is individual, and there are no written documents available. He said the job description is accurate, up to date, and that no one is hired who does not have the qualifications listed on the document. There are two cook shifts (6:00 AM–2:30 PM, and 1:00–9:30 PM) each day, seven days a week. Cooks rotate through both shifts and all are trained for both shifts. Chef Paul says the shifts are "pretty routine" except when there are special events going on. He feels that if cooks are well trained for the regular routine, they will be able to follow his directions for special events without additional training.

JOB DESCRIPTION:

    Job Title: Cook

    Supervisor: Executive Chef or Sous Chef

    General Summary: Prepare menu items for The Garden Room, conferences, room service, and special events

PRINCIPAL DUTIES AND RESPONSIBILITIES:

1. Prepare, cook, assemble, and plate menu items as per the directions of the Chef or Sous Chef.
2. Clean all preparation areas throughout the day.
3. Leave walk-in and dry storeroom neat and clean, with leftovers labeled and dated.
4. All pans, cooking utensils, cooking areas, and equipment (including range, ovens, steam kettle, etc.) must be left clean at shift's end.
5. Put away stock and take inventory at the direction of the Chef or Sous Chef.

REQUIRED KNOWLEDGE, SKILLS, AND ABILITIES:

1. Must be able to work well with entire kitchen staff
2. Must be able to follow the direction of the Chef or Sous Chef
3. Must be able to work fast and efficiently while maintaining high quality standards

EDUCATION AND EXPERIENCE:

1. Must be able to read and write at tenth grade level.
2. Must be able to follow recipes.
3. Must have basic cooking skills.
4. Must have equivalent of one year full-time experience cooking in any forum.

Interview with a Cook

We will interview one cook in depth and check the interview results with the Sous Chef, who was previously a cook, and the Chef. If there is a discrepancy between the Cook, Sous Chef, and Chef, we will interview an additional cook. We asked both the Sous Chef and the Chef which cooks were most representative of the job being done exactly as it should be. They agreed that Tasha was the most talented and creative of all the cooks, but that Andi was closest to the ideal. It was arranged for Andi to come in on her day off and spend three-plus paid hours to help us analyze the cook's job. Andi will be reminded of the purpose of needs assessment and again reassured that she is not being evaluated, and that we need her help in the design of training that will perfectly match the job.

Questions for Andi:

1. What time do you arrive at work?
2. What time are you scheduled to begin work?
3. What are your job duties?
4. What do you do first?
5. What time do you do it?
6. What do you do after that?

(Keep asking questions and assemble a list of sequential duties. Show Andi the list and get her input. Is there anything else that she does that is not on the list? Ask about both cooking shifts. Note the time her breaks/lunch or dinner occur.)

For each duty on the job list, we will ask Andi step-by-step how she does it. We will use the following form for each duty and write the step, how to do it, the performance standard (how we determine if the standard is met, such as comparing the table setting to a picture of how it is to be done), and how long it takes to do it.

Duty:			Total Time:
Step	**Procedure**	**Performance Standard**	**Time**
Step 1			
Step 2			
Step 3			
Step 4			
Step 5			
Step 6			

We will then ask Andi:

1. How were you trained for this job?
2. Were there any duties for which you did not receive training that you should have?

3. Was there any training for duties that you really did not need?

4. What was particularly effective about the way you were trained?

5. What would you change in the training?

6. Are there any parts of your job that need to be changed or that could be improved?

7. Do the jobs in the kitchen work well together? What about the rest of GTI's departmental jobs? Would you make any changes? If so, what would they be?

Cook Observation

The job list, task analysis, performance standards, and other information about the job will be the results of the interview with Andi. We do not want to assume that this information is complete and totally correct. The entire training program for the cook will be based on this information, so we will want to corroborate our interview findings with other sources.

We will observe Andi doing her job using an observation checklist that we will develop based on task analysis. We will also ask the Sous Chef and Chef to review the job list and task analysis documents for their input. If there are discrepancies between the sources, we will have to determine (perhaps through a joint discussion) the correct duties and procedures.

An **observation checklist** is a list of sequential duties that we will be looking for in the observation. We can check the particular duty as we see it performed. We can also indicate on the checklist whether or not the duty is performed in the sequence and in the same way and time as indicated in the interview. We can note how the performance of job duties for the cook position fit and flow with other positions. The observation checklist is a tool that helps us know what to look for and to give the observation some structure. The purpose of the observation is to note discrepancies between what is said in the interview and what is actually done on the job. The checklist helps us to do this.

CONCLUSION

Every step of the instructional design process takes time and effort, and thus is expensive. A plan is necessary to assure that we obtain the correct information, from the right person, and do it in an efficient manner. To determine the position needs we first must devise a job list (which is similar to a job description, but includes *every* duty). We then break down each duty on the job list into the sequential steps it takes (the procedures) and determine the performance standards. We look for additions or subtractions from the job list, and differences in the way duties are performed by utilizing several different sources and methods for obtaining information. In this chapter, we developed a plan and the instruments for obtaining the information. The next chapter will focus on the implementation of the plan.

KEY WORDS

Performance Standard	Motion Economy
Instructional Design	Dovetailing
Job Analysis	Duty
Training Design	Body Mechanics
Work Simplification	Task
Job List	Observation Checklist

CHAPTER THOUGHT QUESTIONS

1. Review and define position needs from Chapter Three. Describe the process for determining position needs. What information is needed? Where do you find this information? From whom do you find it? How do you find it? What tools do you use to find this information?

2. Define job list, duty, and task, and describe how they are related to each other and what they have to do with training design.

3. Task analysis is tedious work. Please define it, describe the process, and discuss why it is important and why it must be done.

4. Review the concept of triangulation from Chapter Three, and discuss triangulation in task analysis.

5. How are job lists and job descriptions similar and different? In an existing operation we might begin task analysis with the job

description. What would we do in a new operation where there is
no job description?

6. Define performance standards and describe how they are
determined and how we find out what the performance standard
is for any specific duty.

7. Define and describe job simplification and motion economy. Why
are they important, and how do they relate to training design?

8. Think about the route you drive or walk to school, work, or any
place you go regularly. What are alternative routes? Draw little
maps of the routes. Which route is faster, more direct, more
pleasant, and so forth? Is there a better route you could travel?

9. Compare and contrast task analysis with work
simplification/motion economy analysis. Could they be done
together as one process? Why or why not? If yes, how?

10. Discuss why all the numerous steps in instructional design
(training design) are so necessary. Justify the incredible amount of
work that goes into designing good formal training.

6 *Implementing Job Analysis*

OBJECTIVES

We planned job analysis in Chapter Five for an existing operation. The process for new operations is similar except there are no existing employees to interview and/or observe. Instead, we can go through the same process in a similar operation and determine what they do. We can combine that information with information obtained from interviews with management and department heads for the new operation, and then devise job lists and procedures and performance standards. We can design training for the opening just as we would for an existing operation. We would, however, be extremely flexible in order to make changes to the procedures and/or training as necessary.

The purpose of this chapter is to take students through the process of job analysis, following the plan devised in Chapter Five. We will write job lists and do task analysis, analyze the procedures to determine if they can be simplified, and determine performance standards for positions at The Garden Terrace Inn (GTI).

Upon completion of Chapter Six, the student should be able to

- Prepare a list of duties for each position in an operation. (Job List)
- Break down these duties into the sequential steps necessary to perform the duty as required by the operation. (Task Analysis)
- Analyze and modify, if necessary, the way a job should be done using motion economy and work simplification principles.
- Determine the performance standards for each of the duties and steps.

Job List

Andi Barnes, a cook at GTI under Chef Paul, was given a total of three additional paid hours to provide us with information about her job. We met in a small conference room and asked her the questions on our list (see Chapter Five). We used the job description to remind her of duties that she was responsible for but that might not have been a regular part of her day. As we went through her description of her duties, we asked clarification questions and were able to put together the following list:

Turn on the oven

Take food from the walk-in (eggs, sausage, bacon, ham, butter, buttermilk, cheese, green peppers, oranges)

Break eggs

Slice bread

Prepare pancake batter

Slice oranges

Prepare muffin batter

Soak French toast in milk and eggs

Precook bacon, sausage, ham, potatoes

Heat maple syrup

Put food on serving platters and bowls for the breakfast buffet

Cook-to-order eggs and omelets

Keep buffet stocked with fresh food

Put away leftovers—labeled and dated

Clean range and line—break down the line to be ready for lunch

Bring in firewood and start fire in grill

Make onion soup

Make soup of the day

Slice cheese, luncheon meats

Make quiche of the day

Make spinach pies

Clean salad

Prepare salad dressings

Cut up beef for brochettes

Stock cooking line for lunch

Prepare garnish

Make croutons

Shred cheese for onion soup

Prepare chicken and tuna salads

Assemble and cook-to-order lunch items

Clean cooking line and put away leftovers

Prepare yeast dough and make bread

Cut steaks, medallions, and brochettes

Cut salmon and halibut

Clean shrimp

Prepare sauces

Prepare rice

Prepare potatoes

Prepare vegetable casseroles

Prepare pasta

Cut up vegetables

Prepare garnish

Set up dinner cooking line

Break down and clean cooking line

Clean range

Put away leftovers

Inventory

Put away groceries

(Sanitation)—added later

(Clean convection oven)—added later

We thought this sounded like a lot for just one person to do. Andi laughed and said that it would be except that one person did not really do it all. They worked together as a team—two cooks on each shift and the Chef or Sous Chef. She said that each cook was responsible for being able to do all the things on the list, and that they usually traded off to keep their speed up. She said one cook might do all the starch items and the other all the protein items, and so forth. The Chef generally prepared all the desserts, because that was his favorite thing to do. The Sous Chef had taken over inventory, scheduling, and purchasing under the supervision and direction of Chef Paul. The Chef did the menus and planned all events and daily specials.

Andi looked the list over and thought it was complete. We showed it to the Sous Chef and the Chef. The Sous Chef thought it looked accurate. The Chef mentioned that the cooks trade off cleaning the convection oven each week. He felt it was very important for all the cooks to be able to do everything. He noted that they did not need much training for most of the duties because they were pretty basic, and he only hired cooks who had experience. The Chef said that it was necessary to train his people in sanitation, because he did not want any food-borne illnesses coming out of his kitchen.

Over forty of the fifty-one items on the job list above (we added cleaning the convection oven and sanitation) had to do with number one on the job description: Prepare, cook, assemble, and plate menu items as per directions of the Chef or Sous Chef. The rest were about cleaning, inventory, and putting away groceries. We may do task analysis for each duty on the job list, or we could do task analysis just for items we are going to design training for. The more task analysis we do, the more it costs to design training. It might be beneficial to do task analysis on all the duties for work simplification and motion economy analysis. However, the Chef is satisfied with the methods his people are using and

Andi, when interviewed, also indicated satisfaction with the amount of work. She stated that they, "worked hard and fast, but all cooks were proud of their work . . . and they all felt appreciated."

Categorize Job List

Categories can emerge from the list and help us envision a training program that incorporates instruction for all listed duties. In reviewing the job list we may notice similarities or connections between items. Identifying training methods can be another factor in categorizing items. We incorporate work simplification/motion economy principles and reorganize the list into categories that bring order and structure.

There are no hard and fast rules about training design. We use common sense. This is knowledge we have gained through experience. The drawback to its use in determining training methods, though, is that many of us have never been formally trained and/or taken a class in training design. We may not know what it is. If we employ common sense without knowledge of all training methods available, we may determine that everything is to be learned on the job. And our idea of on-the-job (OTJ) training may be following around another employee.

As we go through the design process, we are utilizing all training design knowledge we have and using it all together. As students, you unfortunately do not have all the knowledge before you begin categorizing the job list. We are presenting the material sequentially because chapters in a text are sequential, but the material is actually utilized simultaneously. Training methods will be presented in depth in a later chapter.

As we review the job list, we notice there are written recipes for seventeen items. A recipe describes in detail the steps and procedures resulting in the menu item. Essentially, a recipe is task analysis. The job specification part of the job description says that any person hired for the cook position must be able to follow recipes and have basic cooking skills. That means we do not have to train anyone to cook or follow recipes. Our training will involve finding ingredients and supplies, sanitation procedures, plating, and obtaining quality standards.

Other categories become apparent. As we categorize, we eliminate duplication and group duties that are neatly related to be taught together. The following is a reorganized job list grouped into categories that emerged from the list.

Cooking Recipes:
- Prepare pancake batter
- Prepare muffin batter
- Soak French toast in milk and eggs
- Cook to order eggs and omelets
- Make onion soup
- Make soup of the day
- Make quiche of the day
- Make spinach pies
- Prepare salad dressings
- Cut up beef for brochettes
- Make croutons
- Prepare chicken and tuna salads
- Prepare sauces
- Prepare rice
- Prepare potatoes
- Prepare vegetable casseroles
- Prepare pasta

Meat and Fish Cutting:
- Cut steaks, medallions, and brochettes
- Cut salmon and halibut

Prep:
- Break eggs
- Slice bread
- Slice oranges
- Precook bacon, sausage, ham, potatoes
- Heat maple syrup
- Slice cheese, luncheon meats
- Clean salad
- Clean shrimp
- Prepare garnishes

- Shred cheese for onion soup
- Cut up vegetables
- Assemble and cook to order lunch items
- Bring in firewood and start fire in grill
- Turn on the oven

Setting Up Cooking Lines and Breakfast Buffet:
- Put food on serving platters and in bowls for the breakfast buffet
- Keep buffet stocked with fresh food
- Stock cooking line for lunch
- Set up dinner cooking line

Cleaning:
- Clean and break down the line
- Clean the range
- Clean the convection oven

Storage and Inventory:
- Take food from the walk-in
- Put away leftovers—label and date
- Put away groceries
- Inventory

Sanitation:
- Hand-washing
- Cross-contamination
- Time/temperature procedures
- HACCP standards and procedures

Task Analysis

The categorized job list is easier to understand. We shared the reorganized list with the Chef and Sous Chef who both thought it made sense. We obtained copies of the standardized recipes for all items in the "Recipes" section of the job list. (We do not need task analysis when there is a written recipe.) We then set up another meeting with Andi to do task analysis and identify performance standards.

We will begin with "meat and fish cutting" items on the job list and ask Andi questions similar to those we asked while compiling the list. We will say something like, "You are going to cut steaks—so, what do you do first?" She might respond, "I get tenderloins from the walk-in." Then we might ask, "How do you know how many to use?" and so forth until we have a step-by-step breakdown of the task. For some steps the performance standard is the same as the procedure. For other steps, measurable standards can be specified such as, "the steaks should be two inches thick, weigh eight ounces, and have no more than a quarter inch fat on any outside edge."

We will complete a task analysis form for each duty on the job list. The information will be used later as *content* for the lesson plan. We will also use the form when we observe Andi performing her job, and we will check off items as she does them. If steps are performed that were not listed on the form, we will add them and then check with the Chef, Sous Chef, and Andi, confirming that the extra steps are really necessary. We will also note any steps that are not done and go through the same verification check to assure that we have an accurate job list and task analysis. Again, the point is to make sure that the training we design matches the duty perfectly. We do not want to train someone to do the task incorrectly or unrealistically.

Task Analysis Example

Let us imagine we are going to design instruction for making a cup of tea. "Making a cup of tea" is the duty. We must then break this down into sequential steps and identify the performance standard. If we have made many cups of tea, we may deem this exercise a waste of time: "The task is so simple that everyone knows how to do it." This is, however, an assumption that we do not want to make. Not everyone has made tea. And, even if they have made tea before, do they make it the way we want them to make it?

"Pour boiling water over a tea bag and let it steep" may seem like reasonable directions for making tea. On the other hand, if someone has not made tea before . . . the following questions should be answered. How do you boil water? How much water do you boil? How high should the heat be? How long does it take to boil water? Where do you get the water to boil? How much tea do you use? Where do you get the tea? Do you use a tea bag? Does it need to be unwrapped? Do you make the tea in a bowl, a pot, or a cup? How long does the tea steep? What does "steep" mean?

Does the cup need to be covered? What do you do with the tea bag after the tea has steeped?

Duty: Make a Cup of Tea

Total Time: 5 min. 12 sec.

Step	Procedure	Performance Standard	Time
Step 1	Pour 1½ cup bottled water into the stainless steel teakettle.		5 sec.
Step 2	Place teakettle on range and ignite burner directly under teakettle to highest setting.		2 sec.
Step 3	While water is heating, place one white mug from the rack over the sink onto counter by the range.		2 sec.
Step 4	Take one tea bag from the canister labeled "tea" and remove the outer paper wrapper. Discard the wrapper.		3 sec.
Step 5	Place tea bag in mug with the paper square at string's end dangling outside.		1 sec.
Step 6	Allow water in kettle to come to a full boil until kettle begins to whistle.		Aprox. 3 min.
Step 7	Pour boiling water into mug over tea bag to within ½" from top.		2 sec.
Step 8	Cover mug with a saucer and let stand.	No steam should be escaping the cup	2 min.

(continued)

Duty: Make a Cup of Tea *(cont.)*

Step	Procedure	Performance Standard	Time
Step 9	Take cover off mug and remove tea bag. Do not squeeze excess liquid from bag.	Squeezing the bag causes bitterness in tea. Clean up any drips on the cup or counter top	2 sec.
Step 10	Throw used tea bag in the garbage. Voila! The tea is ready.	The tea is steaming hot, dark brown and clear.	1 sec.

To novice instructional designers, this sometimes seems excessive. Do we really need all ten steps to make a simple cup of tea? The answer is, YES. Have you ever tried following the directions for hooking up a VCR or computer? Good directions are easy to follow. Poorly written directions raise questions and cause frustration. If we are attempting to do something new to us, the directions must be accurate and complete.

An experienced cook will know how to assemble a recipe with minimal directions. An inexperienced cook will not. A person used to working with mechanical equipment may have no trouble starting a lawn mower, regardless of whether or not instructions were provided. Someone who is not familiar, though, will need accurate step-by-step directions because they have no applicable experience to carry them into a new situation. Detailed instructions enable us to avoid questions and problems when someone may not be there to answer or solve them. An experienced cook can skim over recipe directions and modify the way he or she would proceed, or they may have their own method validated. Either way, complete accurate directions, when followed, will result in a desired standard.

To determine that directions are complete and accurate, we must have someone try them (pilot test). In that way, we discover whether we have forgotten anything or whether any of the instructions are confusing or unclear. Similarly, if we obtain step-by-step instructions for performing a task on the job list, we can check for accuracy and completeness by then watching the person perform that task while noting differences between what they say and do. We can also cross-check task analysis by sharing it with the worker's manager or supervisor. What is their opinion? If there are discrepancies between sources, we can make further inquiries to assure a consensus on what it should be.

The Garden Terrace Inn Task Analysis: Cook

We asked Andi how she cut the beef for steaks, medallions, and brochettes, then entered data on the task analysis form to be verified through observation and cross-checking with the Chef.

Duty: Cut Steaks, medallions, and brochettes			Total Time: 17 min.
Step	**Procedure**	**Performance Standard**	**Time**
Step 1	Get sanitized cutting board, 12" slicing knife, steel, ounce scale, small sheet pan, baking pan, 2 qt. bowl, and plastic wrap		2 min.
Step 2	Take full beef tenderloin from walk-in, unwrap, and place on cutting board		2 min.
Step 3	Cut 1.5" cubes from ends of the tenderloin and place in bowl	Uniform shape, no fat or gristle	3 min.
Step 4	Cut medallions .25" thick from narrower ends of tenderloin	6 medallions weigh exactly 6 oz., uniformly shaped, and have no fat or gristle	3 min.
Step 5	Cut 1.5" steaks from center of the tenderloin, weighing 6 oz. each	Steaks weigh exactly 6 oz. and are uniform in shape (no thinner than 1.5")	3 min.
Step 6	Cover steaks & medallions with plastic wrap and refrigerate on top shelf. Prepare brochettes (see recipe)		2 min.
Step 7	Weigh and chart any scraps, wrap in plastic and refrigerate		2 min.

Observation

We can analyze tasks and then observe for an entire day or portions of several days, or observe some tasks individually. In the case of cutting meat and fish, we decided to observe after doing task analysis. Andi said she would be cutting meat after lunch the next day, so we told her to call us when she was ready to start. We used the task analysis form as an observation checklist, then stood near where she worked and listed details we observed that were not mentioned in the interview. We questioned some of the things she was doing, and Andi clarified her actions. We then gave the task analysis form to the Chef and asked him if there was anything we missed or anything that was inaccurate or needed clarification. He said that Andi did the task exactly as he wanted it done.

Task Analysis for Remaining Cook Duties on Job List

We go through all remaining duties on the job list with Andi, asking what steps there are for each task. We write them on the task analysis form and then observe her actually doing them. Afterward, we run the results by the Chef and Sous Chef to make sure we have not missed anything. This is not so much difficult as it is tedious.

One of the job list tasks is to break eggs. These eggs are used in omelets or cooked-to-order, added as ingredients for pancake batter, French toast, and the like. Directions for breaking eggs are not included in any recipes. It probably does not matter if we are breaking one egg, but it does matter if we are breaking 120 eggs and time is limited. So, we ask Andi how she does it. We ask her how she determines how many to break, what equipment she uses, and how she sets herself up for the task. We ask her what she does with the broken shells after removing the eggs.

Duty: Break eggs			Total Time: <10 min.
Step	Procedure	Performance Standard	Time
Step 1	Get large metal bowl off shelf and 4 flats of eggs from walk-in.		2 min.
Step 2	Set bowl on counter and place two flats stacked either side, in line with counter's front edge.		Combine this step with step 1

Step	Procedure	Performance Standard	Time
Step 3	Using both hands, grasp the eggs in the two top inner corners of flats on both sides of bowl.		Step 3, 4, & 5 take 3 seconds
Step 4	Lift eggs and rap them firmly against the right and left outer sides of bowl to crack both shells.		
Step 5	Move eggs over the bowl, squeeze gently while forcing them apart allowing eggs to drop into bowl (while holding onto the shells).	Do not let any shells fall into the eggs. Do not allow any of the yolks to break.	
Step 6	Return broken shells to flats and move both hands outward to grasp next two eggs. Keep repeating steps 1–6 until all eggs are broken. Exchange flats when eggs in top flats are broken.		< 6 min.
Step 7	Cover bowl with plastic wrap and return to walk-in, top shelf.		30 seconds
Step 8	Throw flats and shells into the garbage and wipe up and sanitize any egg spills.		1 min.

Conclusion

Task analysis asks the questions, what do we do, how do we do it, what do we do first, how, what do we do next, how, and so forth until the task is completed for each item on the job list. We can apply work simplification and motion economy principles as we verify steps and performance standards with the various sources from whom we have obtained data. Task analysis is time consuming but not difficult. If we keep in mind the purpose, which is to identify every step and everything a person performing the duty must do to complete the task, we can then ask appropriate questions that will result in this information.

We need all these steps so that we can design training that is complete. We do not want our training to be needlessly confusing.

CHAPTER THOUGHT QUESTIONS

1. If you were asked to design training for the housekeeper position at a hotel that had been in operation for five years, please describe the steps you would take to get to the point where you could write a job list. Discuss organization, individual, and position needs.

2. Describe your plan for job analysis for the example in question 1. Discuss what you would need to find out, from whom, and what method you would use to find the information you would need to write a job list for the housekeeping position.

3. How and with whom would you cross-check the information you collected in question two to result in an accurate job list?

4. How and where could you incorporate work simplification and motion economy principles into the above example?

5. Once you have an accurate job list for the housekeeping position, describe how, why, and with whom you would do task analysis.

6. Using the blank Task Analysis Form on the next page, please do a complete task analysis for the following duties. Incorporate work simplification motion economy principles, and be sure to include performance standards. (You may need more or fewer steps than included.)

   - Making a pot of coffee.
   - Wrapping a book to give as a present.
   - Tying a man's necktie.
   - Tying a shoelace.
   - Listing directions to the grocery store nearest your house.

Duty:			**Total Time:**
Step	**Procedure**	**Performance Standard**	**Time**
Step 1			
Step 2			
Step 3			
Step 4			
Step 5			

7 Training Methods and Adult Learning Principles

OBJECTIVES

The results of task analysis provide us with content for training. In order to develop a plan, though, we need an idea of what particular segments of the training will look like in order to arrange them appropriately in the plan. By reorganizing job list tasks into categories according to content and training methods, we can begin to visualize how they could be arranged. In Chapter Six, we reorganized and categorized the job list for the cook position assuming student knowledge of training methods. So, it is in this chapter that we examine various methods that can be utilized for teaching new employees content determined in task analysis.

Upon completion of Chapter Seven, the student should be able to

- List and describe various training methods available for training positions in the hospitality industry.
- Match appropriate training methods for particular training contents.
- List and describe adult learning principles and discuss how they can be incorporated into training programs.

How Adults Learn

Training is different from education. In training, everyone must attain the standard. The standard is an "A," and anything less than that fails. An average mark is not acceptable in training. Seventy percent is generally the cut-off for a "C." Can you imagine only 70 percent of all service encounters being successful? That implies the remaining customers were dissatisfied. It is management's responsibility to make sure every employee masters the material and attains standards. If an employee does not, it is management's responsibility to do more and better until it happens. Our job as instructional designers is to design effective training that assures mastery for every employee.

We choose training methods that will result in the most efficient and effective transferal of job expertise. This has to do with how individuals learn best. We need to understand adult learning principles and motivation in order to choose the best training methods.

Many of our employees enter the hospitality industry by accident rather than by design. Most line employees will not have college degrees and may have had less-than-satisfactory learning experiences in public school. Some employees may be afraid of failing in an educational forum. If training looks, feels, and is structured like "school," many employees could feel threatened. As a result, their level of success could be less than desirable. An informal atmosphere in which employees feel respected and appreciated as professionals—as colleagues—is preferred. Our trainees will need feedback as to how well they are doing, but not in the form of grades assigned in school. They need encouragement ("Yes, that is it!" or, "Good job!") and immediate positive corrective feedback ("Good start! Now, move this a little higher," etc.). The idea is not to catch employees doing something wrong, but to be constantly guiding them toward doing the task correctly.

Encouraging competition among trainees is probably not an effective strategy for bringing out the best results. We want to foster team effort and trust among employees and between employees and management as well. The trainer's attitude toward employees will determine whether or not they feel safe about requesting extra practice or help in mastering material. Our employees will learn at different speeds, and we must determine their progress while allowing them individual time to learn. The objective is competency at the end of training. To meet the objective is the point, and we do whatever is necessary to enable all employees to succeed. Naturally, that may not be the same thing for each employee.

Unlike children, adults have to want to learn something. If they see no point to it, they will not bother. Despite the instructional usefulness of the tea-making exercise earlier, no adult would take it seriously if told to study it. They would say, "Tea's tea," or, "Who cares about tea? Whadaya, nuts?" How much time are we willing to give to something we do not value? Students who do not like math will say, "I will never use algebra." It comes as no surprise that these individuals often do poorly in algebra classes. People who say, "I am not mechanical," or, "I can kill any houseplant," or, "I cannot cook," are usually not deficient—but, rather, they are simply not interested. Therefore, they do not take the time to pay attention and figure out how to do whatever it is that is required of them. If we expect employees to learn how to do something, we must first explain *why* they need to learn it. Explain its importance and how it will benefit them later.

Adults also need to see the "big picture" first. They need to know what it is we want them to do or accomplish (and why) and then have steps sequentially presented to them so it all makes sense. They would prefer not to muddle around in the dark, trusting that things will click at some later date.

Adults have lots of life experience, and if training examples can be related to that, employees will grasp them faster and better. They will also respond more effectively to real examples than to less specific or tangible ones. They should be encouraged to share their own related experiences.

Most adults learn better by doing. So much of our education has been delivered via lectures that we may consider lecturing the best way to convey information. Lectures, however, are one of the least effective methods of instruction. Because all our trainees must attain the standard, we will do very little lecturing. We will do more demonstrating with trainees, who will then practice the activities themselves (with the trainer's immediate positive corrective feedback so they do not practice the activity incorrectly). We will help them to do activities correctly first and then allow them to build up speed naturally. Our training sessions will never be more than forty minutes in length. We will have numerous shorter sessions and build on previous learning. Repetition and practice help adults to remember. There should be very little lag time between initial learning and use of the material.

Adults learn best when they have received material in several different ways. If they hear it, see it, and then do it themselves, it is more likely to be retained. The training itself must be as interesting and relevant as possible. The trainer must be well prepared and attuned to the environment he or she is creating. The trainer must be aware of the relationships and attitudes of trainees. It is the trainer's responsibility to create a positive learning environment and to enthusiastically and effectively deliver training to employees.

Training Methods

Many of us experienced primarily the "lecture" method in school and the "follow around" method on the job. Neither method is the ideal method for learning. The lecture method is convenient and the least expensive. At its worst, one professor can deliver a lecture to a classroom of 400 or more students. The bell curve will definitely be apparent when grades come out. Most students will get Cs. The smallest equal number will get As and Fs, and an equal number will get Bs and Ds. Obviously it is not appropriate for training where everyone needs the equivalent of an A.

Grade school teachers are generally trained to use a variety of methods and to keep lessons fairly short and user-involved. College students would be better served by similar teaching methods. Many professors are not trained to deliver instruction, thus, they do not really know how. They use methods they experienced in their own education. The same thing happens in hospitality training. Unless a trainer personally experienced formal training (structured with a written plan and materials designed to meet specific objectives), or took a course in how to design training, they would probably not know how to train and subsequently would use methods experienced personally on the job. As a result, many new hires are following existing employees around.

Employees can learn the job by following another employee around for a few shifts. However, it is not the most efficient and effective method for learning duties required for the specific job. Think about new servers trying to learn how to take orders by standing behind or next to an experienced server. First of all, is the experienced server actually taking the order in the way the house prefers? The server may answer customer questions about menu items or preparations. What if all questions are not asked in the observed server/customer interaction? How does the new server learn the correct responses? Does he say, "I am new here. I will have to ask." Eventually a new server would most likely experience and learn everything, but at what cost and in how much time?

In the follow-around mode, servers are using the "discovery" method, which can be good education. The discovery method is where teachers provide students with problems and direction and allow students to seek out answers. It can be a thought-provoking experience that fosters thinking and analyzing skills. However, in a training situation we really do not want our new servers discovering answers during service encounters with customers. We want them to already know the answers and provide customers with the service they expect, whether they are new on the job or have been on the job for years. It is not written on the menu that customers can expect inferior service from new servers, and they are not charged less for deficient service. They just do not come back.

We are familiar with the follow-around training method. What do we do, though, in a new facility without experienced employees to follow? The only difference with training in a new or existing facility should be the number of employees being trained. We will be training the entire staff in a new facility and perhaps just one new server or cook in an existing facility. The training we deliver to the new employee or employees should, however, be the same.

We will be using a variety of methods in training because certain methods work better for particular information. We obviously need to be aware of all available methods (and their strengths and weaknesses) in order to make the best possible choices. These methods are backed with written plans and instruction. A trainee may not be aware of the written plan and instruction, just like the audience for a play is not aware of the script the actors are following. If the actors did not follow a script the play could be different each showing. We have a service standard. The menu item or service style is not to differ from time to time. It is to be the standard, always. A "Big Mac" is supposed to look and taste like a "Big Mac" no matter which McDonalds we get it at or at what time we order it. There's no improvisation in standards.

The Demonstration Method

The demonstration method is widely used in hospitality training because many of the duties we are training our new employees to do are **psycho-motor**, that is, the learner must execute some type of muscular activity to achieve particular results. An example of a psycho-motor activity might be setting a table, loading a dish-rack, or preparing a menu item. In a **demonstration** the trainer actually performs the task for the learners while explaining all steps. For a demonstration to be most effective, the learners, following the demonstration, should attempt the task themselves with immediate corrective feedback from the trainer.

There are four steps in a demonstration:

1. We tell the trainee what we want them to do.

2. We show the employee exactly how to do it.

3. We let the employee try to do it and give immediate corrective feedback.

4. We monitor future performance, making sure the employee continues to do it exactly as they learned initially in the training.

We use a lesson plan for demonstration, which is essentially a script. The demonstration is carefully planned so that the trainer is demonstrating the activity exactly as it is to be done, including the steps, the standards, and the explanations we have predetermined to need inclusion. Following the plan assures that every employee who experiences the demonstration gets exactly the same thing and is shown the correct method.

Demonstrations work well for small groups or an individual. To be effective, the demonstration must be very visible. Videotaped demonstrations can be useful, effective, and convenient. However, some type of follow-up activity (such as a supervised practice session) should be planned. Some of us can learn from reading and following written instructions. Most people, though, learn best by listening, watching, and doing. We must remember our responsibility, as instructional designers, to design training that results in mastery of the material for all trainees. We will look at lesson plans for demonstrations in a later chapter.

Simulations

We do not want servers-in-training to practice on our customers. Instead, we can develop simulations for them to practice in a situation representing the real thing. Astronauts practice space flight in simulators before ever leaving Earth. A waiter trainee can practice taking orders from parties comprised of other servers, the trainer, and a manager. Servers can ask the trainee menu questions they probably will have to answer, or provide other service situations they'll eventually have to deal with.

The simulation allows trainees to experience the "real" thing, but without real customers, thus allowing the trainee to make and correct mistakes that will not harm our business. A **simulation** is a contrived situation that looks like a real situation where trainees can safely practice and hone their new service skills before dealing with the public. We generally use the simulation for practicing and testing rather than initial instruction.

We may choose to set up a front desk check-in simulation to allow trainees to practice registering guests. Once they have mastered procedures, and are comfortable with situations that can arise when dealing with customers, they can then do the real job and will not ever have to say, "Please, bear with me. It is my first day on the job."

Role Plays

Role plays are similar to simulations. A **role play** is an instructional method that allows trainees to act out situations under the trainer's direction. Role plays are particularly useful for situations involving the interaction of two or more people, such as handling upset customers. Trainees can be taught certain techniques and then be given a situation where they are to utilize these techniques in a made-up dialogue. Trainees may also be given prepared scripts where they act out parts in an ineffective manner and then in an effective manner. The differences can then be discussed.

Role plays give those involved an awareness of both sides and how one's actions and words affect the other. They can help us become better communicators. Most employees who have customer interactions as the main part of their jobs, such as servers and front desk, are usually somewhat verbal and outgoing to begin with. They generally will enjoy the role play instruction, and it can be a very effective method for honing communication skills.

Role plays will not be an effective means for teaching most kitchen activities. However, managers-in-training might be given role plays to practice directing the behaviors of kitchen employees. "How to handle an insubordinate dishwasher or cook" could be practiced with the role play method. Role plays, like simulations, are generally used to practice and test rather than for initial instruction.

Lectures

We have already covered some weaknesses of the lecture method. However, lecture, when used with other methods, can be very effective if well prepared. A **lecture** is a semiformal presentation by a teacher or trainer verbally telling students or trainees about something.

A lecture that utilizes learning principles, followed with demonstration and practice, or a simulation or role play, can prepare trainees to excel in follow-up learning activities and to understand the importance of what they will be practicing. Lecture by itself, followed with the question, "Do you understand?" may result in a verbal "yes" but an action "no." Again, our responsibility is to make sure everyone masters the material. Lecture by itself may not result in mastery.

Self-Instructional Activities

Some instructional activities can be for trainees to do on their own. We can provide materials, instruction, guidelines, and activities. Managers-in-training sometimes are given a workbook for self-study (under direction of an assigned mentor or trainer). Self-instructional materials can be in the form of interactive computer programs, workbooks, or worksheets. Self-instructional programs can either have prescribed deadlines or be self-paced.

We might use self-instructional activities in hospitality training for such things as learning the menu, sanitation rules, company policies, and so forth. **Self-instructional activities** as a method is a structured lesson or lessons that trainees follow themselves. It includes directions, instructions, activities, materials, and possibly self-quizzes and deadlines.

We never hand an employee a menu and say, "Learn this." If we want an employee to learn the menu using a self-instructional activity, we could provide a workbook or worksheets that describe each menu item, the prices, preparations, substitutions, etc., and there would be a series of self-check questions for the trainee to work through. We then must augment the self-instructional portion with some type of follow-up activity that brings the message home—perhaps a service encounter simulation where the trainee has to use information from the workbook to answer customer questions about the menu.

We might have employees view a video demonstration of proper hand-washing techniques. At the same time, they might fill out a worksheet that forces them to list the steps they observed in the video. The self-instructional portion would be followed with supervised practice of proper hand-washing. We often utilize a combination of methods because learning is easier when information is presented in several different ways.

Classroom Methods

It may be convenient to conduct some training activities in a classroom setting. We can hold lectures, discussions, question and answer sessions, and conduct role plays in a private room away from customers and distractions. We may set up simulations in a classroom so that we are not disturbing customers. We may also do other sorts of learning activities such as written exercises.

If we were trying to train servers to write checks, we might use a chalkboard or overhead projector to show examples. We might provide handouts that have the check order next to each written menu item, and then have another handout with the check orders left blank for trainees to fill in. We might lecture on how to post dinner charges to guest rooms, show trainees how to fill out appropriate paperwork, and then give them problems to do.

Prepared Training Materials

There are already prepared training materials available from many sources. There is no benefit to preparing our own materials if ready prepared materials are appropriate. Videos, training manuals, self-instructional materials, and interactive computer training programs can be purchased and used as-is or modified to perfectly match a particular operation.

We might choose to send an employee to a workshop or seminar for specialized training. Sanitation is often taught by county health departments. Cake-decorating or customer service (or any number of topics) can be covered by someone other than us and may be a good training option for our operation.

On-The-Job Training

We often think, incorrectly, of **on-the-job training** (OTJ) as following someone around for a shift or two. OTJ is, instead, planned structured training conducted on the actual job site. There are written objectives, content, and procedures. OTJ follows the plan so that any employee going through training would receive the same instruction. The trainer would probably be the experienced employee doing the job, and they would have been formally trained to conduct OTJ. Trained to follow the plan and cover all points and procedures as per design.

OTJ can be similar to a demonstration, but, rather than "staged" specifically for training, the demonstration might occur as it is actually unfolding on the job. OTJ can be structured practice with a regular employee of duties the trainee learned with other methods. OTJ might utilize checklists for the trainee to follow as the regular employee performs job duties.

Training Methods— The Garden Terrace Inn

Let us select training methods for items on the job list for the cook position. We have to keep in mind the job specification qualifications on the job descriptions. The cook is to have at least one year of cooking experience and know how to follow recipes. That means that our training does not cover basics such as measuring and cooking techniques.

For recipes on the job list, we will not be teaching new cooks to prepare pancakes or muffins. They can follow the recipe. We will have to make sure they know where the recipe is, how much they should prepare, when they should prepare the pancakes, where all the ingredients are, and so forth. All duties in the cooking portion of the job list will most likely be taught OTJ using checklists, recipes, demonstrations, and practice. Where ingredients and utensils are located will also be covered in the inventory and storage training.

Training for setting up cooking lines and the breakfast buffet will most likely be taught OTJ with diagrams of the lines and buffets. Cleaning the oven and range will be taught with OTJ demonstrations.

Storage and inventory will be taught as a classroom activity, occurring, though, in the actual storage areas. A tour with a detailed map of storage areas (combined with lecture and inventory exercises) will be conducted by a trainer. The trainee will do OTJ inventory with an experienced cook at the next inventory.

Sanitation will be taught with a purchased video and self-instructional workbook, a sanitation workshop conducted by the local health department, and weekly in-service reminders OTJ.

Cooking (OTJ training with recipes, checklists, demonstrations, and practice)

Recipes:

- Prepare pancake batter
- Prepare muffin batter
- Soak French toast in milk and eggs
- Cook to order eggs and omelets
- Make onion soup
- Make soup of the day
- Make quiche of the day
- Make spinach pies
- Prepare salad dressings
- Cut up beef for brochettes
- Make croutons

- Prepare chicken and tuna salads
- Prepare sauces
- Prepare rice
- Prepare potatoes
- Prepare vegetable casseroles
- Prepare pasta

Meat and Fish Cutting: (OTJ demonstration and supervised practice)
- Cut steaks, medallions, and brochettes
- Cut salmon and halibut

Prep: (OTJ demonstration and supervised practice)
- Break eggs
- Slice bread
- Slice oranges
- Precook bacon, sausage, ham, potatoes
- Heat maple syrup
- Slice cheese, luncheon meats
- Clean salad
- Clean shrimp
- Prepare garnishes
- Shred cheese for onion soup
- Cut up vegetables
- Assemble and cook-to-order lunch items
- Bring in firewood and start fire in grill
- Turn on the oven

Setting Up Cooking Lines and Breakfast Buffet (OTJ w/diagrams of lines and buffets)
- Put food on serving platters and in bowls for breakfast buffet
- Keep buffet stocked with fresh food
- Stock cooking line for lunch
- Set up dinner cooking line

Cleaning: (OTJ demonstrations)

- Clean and break down line
- Clean range
- Clean convection oven

Storage and Inventory: (Classroom, tour with map, lecture and exercises, and OTJ)

- Take food from the walk-in
- Put away leftovers/label and date
- Put away groceries
- Inventory

Sanitation: (Purchased video and self-instructional workbook, health department workshop, weekly in-services reminders, and OTJ)

- Hand-washing
- Cross-contamination
- Time/temperature procedures
- HACCP standards and procedures

SUMMARY

The Principles of Adult Learning:

a) Trainees prefer an informal atmosphere for sessions where they are treated as professionals rather than students.

b) Trainees need encouragement and positive feedback regarding their progress.

c) Trainees should not be forced to compete with each other.

d) Trainees learn at different speeds and may need individual attention.

e) Trainees must want to learn and understand why the material is necessary.

f) Trainees must be told what they are to do and then be shown the sequential steps to do it.

g)   The training should be related to the trainees' life experiences.

h)   Trainees need real and tangible examples.

i)   Trainees learn better by doing.

j)   Trainees should learn to do the activity correctly, then build up speed.

k)   Training should be conducted in numerous shorter sessions.

l)   Repetition and practice result in better retention.

m)   Lag time should be kept short between training time and the on-the-job use of information.

n)   A combination of training methods should be used.

o)   The training should be made interesting and relevant.

p)   The trainer should be well prepared.

q)   The trainer must create a positive learning environment.

r)   The trainer must exhibit enthusiasm.

The Methods of Teaching:

a)   Demonstration

b)   Simulation

c)   Role Plays

d)   Lecture

e)   Self-Instructional Methods

f)   Classroom Activities

g)   Prepared Training Materials

h)   On-the-Job Training

KEY WORDS

Psycho-motor	Role-play
Demonstration	Lecture
Simulation	On-The-Job Training (OTJ)

CHAPTER THOUGHT QUESTIONS

1. Think about your very favorite class you have attended. Why was it your favorite? What made it so good? How was it taught? What teaching methods did the instructor use?

2. Think about the worst class you have ever had. Why was it the worst? What made it so bad? How was it taught? What teaching methods did the teacher use?

3. Think about a time you enjoyed a class you thought you would not like. If you had a different teacher, do you think you would have liked it as much? What made the class so good? How was it taught? What teaching methods did the teacher use?

4. When it comes to enjoying a class, does it have more to do with the teacher or the material? Discuss and justify your answer.

5. Describe the differences and similarities between teaching adults and children. Please address the Adult Learning Principles, and you may use your own experience for the *teaching children* part of the question.

6. List the eight teaching methods described in your text, and indicate a specific hospitality training situation where each might be a good choice.

7. Think about a current or past job. Describe how you were trained, who trained you, how long it took, and what methods were used. Was it effective? Could it have been improved? How?

8. Describe the difference between shadowing and OTJ training. Discuss the problems with shadowing when it is used as the sole method of training new employees.

9. Why is shadowing such a popular training method in the hospitality industry? What method should be used instead?

10. Training differs from education in that for training we need only teach what employees must know to do the job, and all trainees must master the material. Please discuss strategies for making sure all trainees master the material. Include Adult Learning Principles and training methods in your discussion.

8 *Training Plan*

OBJECTIVES

Once we have determined training needs, and task analysis has been done for each duty on a position's job list, we then develop a training plan (step number two in the Training Design Model).

Step #1	#2	#3	#4	#5	#6	#7
Needs Assessment	Training Plan	Lesson Plans	Trainer Training	Training Implementation	Training Evaluation	Coaching and Counseling

The **training plan** is a well-thought-out detailing of training topics and a schedule of when, where, and by whom they will be presented.

Upon completion of Chapter Eight, the student should be able to

- Prepare a training plan for any hospitality position, which includes defining the trainees and the broad training objectives, selecting the trainer, and determining a training schedule (i.e., where and when segments will take place).

Define the Trainees

In human resources management we are acutely aware of the problems of discrimination. Even if discrimination was not against the law, we would not want to limit our employee possibilities and potentials by making assumptions based on race, gender, nationality, religious, or age grounds.

Generalizations are often incorrect and hurt both the company and the people we are making assumptions about. There is a big difference, however, between defining our labor pool and our labor force.

The job specification describes the qualifications and characteristics necessary for a person to be able to adequately perform in a position. Only people who already have the qualifications and characteristics may be hired for the job. They are then trained to do the principal duties and responsibilities that make up the job description.

Job specification is the required knowledge, skills, and abilities—combined with education and experience—that entail certain parts of the job description. It usually does not include age, gender, race, national origin, or religion. (Note: Bonafide Occupational Qualifiers are legitimate reasons for excluding persons for otherwise illegal considerations, such as specifying gender for bathroom attendants.)

The job specification portion of the job description below for the cook position at GTI specifies that the applicant must be able to "Get along, follow directions, and have cooking experience." The position is open to all ages, gender, race, religion, or nationality. It is not discrimination when we describe people we have already hired. Nor is it wrong to say that of the six full-time cooks, four are men; two are Hispanic; and all are between the ages of twenty-seven and forty. Five of the six cooks graduated from high school, and two of the six attended college.

It would, however, be discrimination if we were to say we hire only Hispanics or Caucasians between the ages of twenty-seven and forty.

We would probably use different language, examples, and activities if we were trying to teach high school students versus, for example, middle-aged women. Our training would look and sound differently if we were trying to teach people whose English was limited. We need to define who our trainees are so that we can design training that matches their learning needs. It does not mean that we will not occasionally have a new employee who does not fit the usual profile. We may have to modify our set training for that individual.

We can, for the most part, design training for the typical profile of that particular job. If we live in an area where there is very limited immigration and most people speak English, it would not make sense to bother designing multilingual training. If, on the other hand, the labor pool had a common disadvantage or need, we would most likely need to design training that addresses that circumstance. We must always be realistic. Our task is to design training that will enable all new-hires to do the jobs as we determine they should be done.

JOB DESCRIPTION:

>Title: Cook

>Supervisor: Executive Chef or Sous Chef

>General Summary: Prepare menu items for The Garden Room,
>conferences, room service, and special events.

PRINCIPAL DUTIES AND RESPONSIBILITIES:

1. Prepare, cook, assemble, and plate menu items as per directions of the Chef or Sous Chef.
2. Clean all preparation areas throughout the day.
3. Leave walk-in and dry storeroom neat and clean, with all leftovers labeled and dated.
4. All pans, cooking utensils, cooking areas, and equipment (including range, ovens, steam kettle, etc.) must be left clean at shift's end.
5. Put away stock and take inventory at Chef or Sous Chef's direction.

REQUIRED KNOWLEDGE, SKILLS, AND ABILITIES:

1. Must be able to work well with entire kitchen staff.
2. Must be able to follow directions of the Chef or Sous Chef.
3. Must be able to work fast and efficiently while maintaining high quality standards.

EDUCATION AND EXPERIENCE:

1. Must be able to read and write at tenth grade level.
2. Must be able to follow recipes.
3. Must have basic cooking skills.
4. Must have equivalent of one year of full-time experience cooking (in any forum).

Training Profile for Cooks at GTI

By assessing our current and past cooks, plus the labor pool from which we hire, we have determined that the typical new cook will be Caucasian or Hispanic and of either sex. They will most likely be a high school graduate between the ages of twenty-five and forty-five who speaks and writes

English. We will design training taking into consideration the needs of this particular group.

Training Objectives

There are objectives at the beginning of each chapter in this text. They state what the student should be able to do upon completion of the chapter. Our broad training objectives state what the trainee will be able to do upon completion of training. These objectives are always **behavioral**. They are stated in action verbs, such as "take orders," not, "*understand* how to take orders," or, "*know* how to take orders." Obviously, they must know and understand in order to be able to take orders, but knowing and understanding does not mean they will actually be able to take orders.

By stating behavioral objectives, we are better able to plan our training to reach these objectives. A test for "to know or understand" something might be a written quiz. A test for "be able to do" would be to actually demonstrate the skill. To teach someone to know or understand could be done with a lecture. To teach someone to do something would perhaps require a demonstration and practice. This is training, not education. We are training our people to do things—not to understand or know. That alone is not enough.

Training objectives get narrower and more specific as we begin designing the actual training segments. We start, however, with the broad training objectives. The broad training objective for the cook position is: "Upon completion of training, the trainee will be able to perform all duties of the cook position as per standards of GTI."

The five training topics or areas for the cook position in Chapter Seven are:

1. Cooking
2. Setting Up Cooking Lines and Breakfast Buffet
3. Cleaning
4. Storage and Inventory
5. Sanitation

Each training topic will have a broad training objective—what the trainee will be able to do upon completion of the training topic. We cannot possibly meet the broad training objective in one session, so we will break the session into numerous segments, each with a narrower and more specific objective. The cooking topic has over eighteen recipes plus preparation of fourteen other items. We will decide how many sessions we need and which recipes and preps should be taught within. Each session will have a behavioral objective.

Topic #1, Cooking: Upon completion of training, the trainee will be able to prepare all the recipes and prep items as per recipes and standards of GTI.

1-a　Upon completion of the training session, the trainee will be able to
1. Slice oranges
2. Slice cheese and luncheon meats
3. Prepare garnish
4. Shred cheese for onion soup as per standards of GTI

1-b　Upon completion of the training session, the trainee will be able to
1. Precook bacon, sausage, ham, and potatoes
2. Heat maple syrup as per standards of GTI

1-c.　Upon completion of the training session, the trainee will be able to
1. Clean salad
2. Clean shrimp
3. Cut up vegetables as per standards of GTI

1-d　Upon completion of the training session, the trainee will be able to
1. Cut steaks, medallions, and brochettes
2. Cut salmon and halibut as per standards of GTI

1-e　Upon completion of the training session, the trainee will be able to
1. Assemble and cook-to-order lunch items
2. Bring in firewood and ignite grill as per standards of GTI

1-f　Upon completion of the training session, the trainee will be able to
1. Break eggs
2. Prepare pancake batter
3. Prepare muffin batter
4. Soak French toast in milk and eggs

    5. Slice bread

    6. Make croutons as per standards of GTI

1-g Upon completion of the training session, the trainee will be able to

    1. Make onion soup

    2. Make soup of the day

    3. Prepare vegetable casseroles as per standards of GTI

1-h Upon completion of the training session, the trainee will be able to

    1. Make quiche of the day

    2. Make spinach pies as per standards of GTI

1-i Upon completion of the training session, the trainee will be able to

    1. Prepare chicken and tuna salads as per standards of GTI

1-j Upon completion of the training session, the trainee will be able to

    1. Prepare sauces

    2. Prepare salad dressings as per standards of GTI

1-k Upon completion of the training session, the trainee will be able to

    1. Prepare potatoes

    2. Prepare pasta

    3. Prepare rice as per standards of GTI

Topic #2, Setting Up Cooking Lines and Breakfast Buffet: Upon completion of the training session, the trainee will be able to set up cooking lines for all meals and stock the breakfast buffet as per standards of GTI.

2-a Upon completion of the training session, the trainee will be able to

    1. Set up cooking line for breakfast

    2. Set up the breakfast buffet

    3. Keep buffet stocked with fresh food

    4. Turn on the oven as per standards of GTI

2-b Upon completion of the training session, the trainee will be able to

    1. Stock cooking line for lunch

    2. Set up dinner cooking line as per standards of GTI

Topic #3, Cleaning: Upon completion of the training session, the trainee will be able to clean specified areas and equipment as per standards of GTI.

3-a Upon completion of the training session, the trainee will be able to
1. Clean and break down line after all three meals as per standards of GTI.

3-b Upon completion of the training session, the trainee will be able to
1. Clean range
2. Clean convection oven as per standards of GTI

Topic #4, Storage and Inventory: Upon completion of the training session, the trainee will be able to store food and supplies in their proper place and take inventory as per standards of GTI.

4-a Upon completion of the training session, the trainee will be able to
1. Take food from walk-in
2. Stow leftovers—label and date
3. Stow groceries as per standards of GTI

4-b Upon completion of the training session, the trainee will be able to
1. Take inventory as per standards of GTI

Topic #5, Sanitation: Upon completion of the training session, the trainee will be able to follow correct sanitation procedures for all activities as per standards of GTI.

5-a Upon completion of the training session, the trainee will be able to
1. Wash hands properly
2. Follow procedures to avoid cross-contamination as per standards of GTI

5-b Upon completion of the training session, the trainee will be able to
1. Follow correct time/temperature procedures
2. Follow correct HACCP procedures as per standards of GTI

Selecting the Trainer

There is a common misconception that teaching is easy and anyone can do it. Most of us have experienced enough bad teachers to realize that some people should definitely not be teaching. The same is true in training. It is important for the trainer to understand the job. The rub is, though, that the trainer is not actually doing the job. They are teaching someone else how to do the job. Teaching the job and doing the job are not the same. They require totally different skills.

Training takes additional time. OTJ training may mean that an employee is working with another employee who is doing the job, but who also has training responsibilities. Employees who have been given these added duties must first be trained to train, and they should also be given additional time to fulfill their second tier of responsibilities.

Trainers have to want to train. Not everyone likes to train. Some might find the extra responsibility burdensome and, if they're servers, they might find the constant shadow a drain on their ability to make optimum money. Some people do not have the patience or social skills to be comfortable training. Others may be expert at their jobs but unable to tell or show others how to do them. Trainers have to be flexible, understanding, and attuned to the people they are instructing.

We determined training methods in Chapter Six for the five training topics. The main type of training will be OTJ. There are a couple different ways to go about this. We could have the trainee work with an employee who will show them what he or she is doing, allowing the trainee to practice within the context of a regular shift. Or, we could have a trainer working with the trainee while another employee does the job. The trainer would be explaining what the regular employee is doing and providing practice for the trainee. This, of course, might be perceived as annoying by customers in a dining experience.

Most employees are very busy, and trying to train someone while doing the job can be trying. The trainee is in the way, and it is hard to let the trainee do anything because it takes longer to explain than to do the job themselves. We can design OTJ training plans and lesson plans. We will have objectives and methods for teaching. There will also be materials (check sheets and practice assignments for the trainee to do while OTJ).

There may be a full-time trainer in very large operations. Most smaller operations, though, will use managers and existing employees for trainers—so, OTJ training will most likely be done by an employee doing the job. It is extremely important to make sure that only capable employees who want to train are given training responsibilities, and then they must be trained to train. (We will deal with training the trainer in a later chapter.)

The GTI Trainers

Our employee questionnaire indicated that half our cooks were interested in training new ones. Because all cooks are cross-trained, we will not have difficulty assigning training responsibilities. The Chef will do classroom sanitation and inventory training and also several of the cooking demonstrations. Below are the five training topics, the methods of training, selected trainers, and where the training will take place.

Training Topic	Training Method	Trainer	Place Held
#1: Cooking	OTJ with recipes, checklists, demonstration and practice	Chef 3 cooks	Kitchen
#2: Setting Up Cooking Lines and Breakfast Buffet	OTJ with diagrams of lines and buffets	3 cooks	Kitchen Dining Room
#3: Cleaning	OTJ demonstration	3 cooks	Kitchen
#4: Storage and Inventory	Classroom, tour with map, lecture and exercises, plus OTJ	Chef 3 cooks	Storage Areas Small Conference Room
#5: Sanitation	Purchased video and self-instructional workbook, health department workshop, OTJ, and weekly in-services reminders	Chef Sous Chef	Small Conference Room Kitchen

Determining the Training Schedule

How long it should take to thoroughly train an employee depends on the employee and the particular job. Loading racks and running and maintaining a dish machine may take less than an hour for thorough training. The cook's position has many more complex duties, however, and could take up to a week to train. We must only hire people who have the qualifications and are capable of doing the job. Because people learn at different speeds, we may lengthen or shorten training time depending on an individual's training needs. It is our responsibility to make sure that new employees attain the standards before they are let loose on the job.

An employee who is in training is not contributing. We want training to be effective and efficient so the employee can be contributing as soon as possible. We must plan the training segments with learning principles in mind. The segments should not be too long or too complex. They should be spaced so that repetition and practice strengthen the skills, and, consequently, these new skills can build on previous ones. We do not want to allow too much lapse time between training and when they will have to do the things they learned therein.

Training Schedule for the Cook at GTI

We have nineteen training segments (1-a–5-b) for the cook that must be organized into the regular work week. There is no formula for determining how long the training should be, but a week seems reasonable. All cooks are required to be proficient at both shifts (AM and PM), so the training will reflect that.

When we observed the cook during the needs assessment phase of training design, we became aware of a sequential schedule. We used this schedule as the basis for arranging training segments. We made a copy of the list of nineteen training sessions and checked off as we pieced them into the existing schedule in a reasonable manner.

New employees may start training on any day of the week, but they will work the same shift as Chef Paul on day number one. The trainee will join Chef Paul for breakfast to experience the breakfast buffet from the guest's perspective, after which Chef will conduct a tour with a detailed explanation of storage. Chef indicated, though (when interviewed during needs assessment), that he felt sanitation was extremely important. To wit we elected to do classroom sanitation instruction early in the training. We will follow with classroom instruction on the menu before getting into preparation. Please see the following schedule and note OTJ sessions are scheduled to occur when workers are normally performing the tasks. When we finished the schedule, we went back over the list and verified that all the segments were included. Once we begin designing the instruction, we may find it necessary to modify the schedule—but, as is, it gives us structure to begin the design phase.

Day 1: 7:00 AM to 3:30 PM

Time		Training Segment	Trainer	Where Held
7:00		Meet Chef/breakfast buffet	Chef	Dining Room
7:20	4a 4b	Tour/storage and inventory	Chef	Storage areas
8:30	5a 5b	Sanitation	Chef	Small Conf. Room
9:30		Menu—recipes	Chef	Small Conf. Room
10:30	3a 1	Break down breakfast line and buffet	Cook	Kitchen and Dining Room
11:00	2b 1	Set up lunch line	Cook	Kitchen
11:30	1e 1	Assemble/cook lunch orders	Cook	Kitchen
1:30		Lunch with Chef	Chef	Dining Room
2:00		Dinner Prep	Cook	Kitchen
3:00	3a 1	Break down and clean lunch line	Cook	Kitchen

Day 2: 6:00 AM to 2:30 PM

Time		Training Segment	Trainer	Where Held
6:00	1f, 1–5 2a 4	Breakfast prep	Cook	Kitchen
	2a 1 2 1 2	Set up breakfast line and buffet Keep buffet stocked	Cook	Kitchen and Dining Room

Time	Training Segment		Trainer	Where Held
8:00	1g 1 1g 2	Prepare Soups	Cook	Kitchen
9:30	5a 5b 4a 4b	Sanitation/Storage and Inventory	Chef	Storage areas
10:30	3a 1	Break down breakfast line and buffet	Cook	Kitchen and Dining Room
11:00	2b 1	Set up lunch line	Cook	Kitchen
11:30	1e 1	Assemble and cook lunch orders	Cook	Kitchen
1:00	1c 1 1j 2 1c 3 1g 3	Clean salad Prepare salad dressings Cut up vegetables Prepare vegetable casseroles	Cook	Kitchen

Day 3: 6:00 AM to 2:30 PM

Time	Training Segment		Trainer	Where Held
6:00	1f 1–5 1b 1 1b 2 1f 6	Breakfast prep	Cook	Kitchen

(continues)

Day 3: 6:00 AM to 2:30 PM *(cont.)*

Time	Training Segment		Trainer	Where Held
	2a 1	Set up breakfast line and buffet	Cook	Kitchen and Dining Room
		Keep buffet stocked		
	2a 2	Prep		
	2a 3			
	1a 1–4			
10:30	3a 1	Break down breakfast line and buffet	Cook	Kitchen and Dining Room
11:00	1e 2	Fire grill	Cook	Kitchen
	2b 1	Set up lunch line		
11:30	1e 1	Assemble and cook lunch orders	Cook	Kitchen
		Work line	Cook	Kitchen
2:00	3b 2	Clean convection oven	Cook	Kitchen

Day 4: 1:00 to 9:30 PM

Time	Training Segment		Trainer	Where Held
1:00		Lunch with Chef	Chef	Dining Room
1:30	1i 1	Prepare chicken and tuna salads	Cook	Kitchen
2:30	1d 1	Cut meat and fish	Chef	Kitchen
	1d 2			

Time	Training Segment		Trainer	Where Held
3:30	1c	Clean shrimp	Cook	Kitchen
	2	Prepare potatoes, pasta, and rice		
	1k	Prepare sauces		
	1–3			
	1j			
	1			
4:00	2b	Set up and stock dinner line	Cook	Kitchen
	1			
	2b			
	2	Work line	Cook	Kitchen
9:00	3b	Clean range	Cook	Kitchen
	1	Break down and clean line		
	3a			
	1			

Day 5: 1:00 to 9:30 PM

Time	Training Segment		Trainer	Where Held
1:00	1h	Prepare quiche and spinach pies	Cook	Kitchen
	1			
	1h			
	2	Dinner prep	Cook	Kitchen
3:30	3a	Break down lunch line	Cook	Kitchen
	1			
4:00	2b	Set up and stock dinner line	Cook	Kitchen
	1			
	2b			
	2	Work line	Cook	Kitchen
9:00	3b	Clean range	Cook	Kitchen
	1	Break down and clean line		
	3a			
	1			

CONCLUSION

Arranging a training schedule is not a high tech endeavor. Through needs assessment we have a good idea of the scope of each segment, we know how we are going to teach each segment, and we know who is going to do the teaching. We are using written lists of the training segments and the sequenced schedule from the observation, and then using our heads to determine the order that makes the most sense. The training schedule can be modified if need be as we begin designing lesson plans.

KEY WORDS

Training Plan   Behavioral Objective

CHAPTER THOUGHT QUESTIONS

1. Think about any class you have taken recently. Was there a training plan or a "learning" plan? How was the class organized? Were you given a syllabus? Were there lesson topics? What similarities are there between planning a class and planning training?

2. For the class you described in question one, describe the typical profile of the students the class was designed for. Were there any students in the class that did not match the profile? Did those who did not match the profile need and/or receive any special instruction or modifications of the instruction?

3. Please discuss the difference between defining the trainees and discrimination.

4. This training textbook has an overall objective of teaching students to design training. The text is broken into fourteen topics or chapters. What is the broad training objective of Chapter Eight? The topic of Chapter Eight is broken into numerous segments, each with a narrower and more specific behavioral objective. What are they?

5. Think about all the teachers you have ever had in school. Which ones did you like the best? What characteristics did they have that made them so good? Think about job training you have experienced. Were there any people who trained you who were particularly good at training? What made them good trainers? Are there similarities between good trainers and good teachers? Do they need similar characteristics? What characteristics should they have to be good trainers?

6. Washing a car is a psycho-motor activity. If you were going to teach a ten-year-old to wash a car, what training method would you use? Where would you do it? How long do you think it would it take to train the child? How would you know whether the child could do it on his or her own?

7. When you are planning the training schedule, list and discuss the factors that you need to take into consideration. Consider this: a single training session from nine AM until one PM. What is wrong with this training schedule?

8. Some students will stay up all night studying for a final exam. Critique this study method in light of the suggestions given in your text for determining the training schedule.

9. Describe the process for developing a training plan. How do you know what to teach first, to whom, how, and by whom?

10. Most of your teachers in school had training or learning plans. Think about all the times you have been trained for a job. Do you know if they had training plans? Do you think they did? If you do not think they did, would a training plan have made the training better? Discuss this.

9 Lesson Plans

OBJECTIVES

All the work to this point has prepared us to finally begin designing instruction. Lesson plans are the actual instruction and are the third step in the Training Design Model.

Step #1	#2	#3	#4	#5	#6	#7
Needs Assessment	Training Plan	Lesson Plans	Trainer Training	Training Implementation	Training Evaluation	Coaching and Counseling

Many of us have experienced training that skipped steps 1–4 and went directly to implementation. Training without planning, though, is inconsistent and grossly ineffective. Well-designed training is expensive, but the cost of unplanned follow-around training is far more pricey in the long run. A lesson plan is essentially a script of the training, coupled with all materials, activities, and instructions needed to meet objectives.

Upon completion of Chapter Nine, the student should be able to

• Develop a lesson plan for any hospitality training segment.

Lesson Plans

We hear of lesson plans for grade school teachers. We hear of substitute teachers coming in and following the absent grade school teacher's lesson plans. We rarely hear about lesson plans at the university level, though.

When was the last time you ever heard about a training lesson plan? All instruction needs a lesson plan. Without a lesson plan, there is no instruction—just some vague idea of what must be taught or trained.

A lesson plan is very much like the script for a play. The script has all the players' parts and all the players' movements (the action). The players could be substituted with other players and they would still say the same words and make the same movements. The new players might not be as talented, but words and movements would be the same. A good lesson plan may be followed by anyone who can read and who has at least a vague understanding of the subject matter. Words and activities would be the same although delivery might not be as smooth.

If a teacher or trainer has an excellent lesson plan, but has delivered the lesson many times, they probably won't need to refer to any actual script. However, it was there initially and served its purpose until the entire lesson was memorized. Written lesson plans allow for training to continue even if the trainer leaves that position. Someone else can step in and fill the former trainer's shoes. During the needs assessment phase of training design we identified all procedures for items on the job list. Procedures are the subject matter in our lesson plans. We will now develop scripts and actions the trainer can follow to deliver subject matter to trainees.

GTI: Lesson Plans for OTJ Training

We could begin developing lesson plans for the first training segment on day number one of the training plan. We will, however, start with day number two because we already have the breakdowns for breaking eggs completed in Chapter Six.

Day #2: 6:00 AM to 2:30 PM

Time	Training Segment		Trainer	Where Held
6:00	1f 1–5 2a 4	Breakfast prep	Cook	Kitchen

The Training Segment is for Breakfast Prep and includes 1.f.1–5. and 2.a.4. The objectives for the training segment were identified in Chapter Eight as follows:

1f: Upon completion of the session the trainee will be able to

1)   Break eggs

2)   Prepare pancake batter

3)   Prepare muffin batter

4)   Soak French toast in milk and eggs

5)   Slice bread as per standards of GTI

2a.4. Turn on the oven

Breaking eggs is one of the items on the cook's job list at GTI, and it is the first lesson in the training segment. The task was broken down into eight steps in Chapter Six. We are scheduled to train a new cook to break eggs (1.f.1.) on day number two between six and seven AM. We identified the training method in Chapter Seven as OTJ with demonstration and practice. The trainer is the cook on duty who has indicated an interest in training new hires. The training will take place within the context of the usual breakfast prep. The trainer will have received training in how-to-train prior to conducting the Breakfast Prep training.

Lesson Plan—Breakfast Prep

1.f.1. Break Eggs

Time: @ six AM

Place: Kitchen

Trainer: Breakfast Cook

Method: OTJ and Demonstration and Practice

Duration: Ten minutes

Objective: Upon completion of the training session, the trainee will be able to break eggs as per standards of GTI.

Step	Procedure	Trainer's Directions
Step 1	Get large metal bowl and four flats of eggs from the walk-in.	"We are going to break enough eggs for pancakes, muffins, French toast, and all the egg dishes we will be preparing to order. Come with me and I will show you where to get the eggs and equipment we need for this." [Take trainee to the

Step	Procedure	Trainer's Directions
		walk-in and pick up the eggs, then go to the bowl rack and get a large metal bowl.]
Step 2	Set bowl directly in front of yourself on counter and place two egg flats stacked on either side of bowl, all in line with the front of counter.	"We want to set ourselves up so we can work efficiently and comfortably, like this." [Explain and do step number two.]
Step 3	Using both hands, grasp eggs in the two top inner corners of flats on both sides of bowl.	"Now I am going to show you how we break two eggs at a time . . . then you are going to practice by breaking the rest."
Step 4	Lift eggs from flats and rap firmly against right and left outer sides of bowl, cracking both eggshells.	"You see how I am making my hands work together rhythmically and fast. It takes a quick sharp rap to break the eggs."
Step 5	Move eggs over the bowl and squeeze gently while forcing them apart, allowing the eggs to fall into the bowl while holding onto the shells.	"We do not let any shell fall into the bowl. Also, try to avoid breaking any of the yolks."
Step 6	Return broken shells to flats and move both hands outward to grasp next two eggs. Keep repeating steps 1–6 until all eggs are broken. Exchange flats when eggs in top are all broken.	[Explain steps while physically demonstrating for the trainee. Then trade places and have them break two eggs. Give corrective feedback and allow the trainee to finish breaking the remaining eggs.]
Step 7	Cover the bowl of eggs with plastic wrap and return it to the walk-in top shelf.	[Explain step number seven and show trainee where the plastic wrap is, how the bowl should be covered, and where it goes in the walk-in.]
Step 8	Throw flats and shells in garbage and wipe up and sanitize any egg spills.	[Explain and demonstrate step number eight.] "We want to be very careful to avoid cross-contamination with the raw eggs. We wipe up any spills and then sanitize." [Demonstrate.]

Evaluation: On day number three of training, have the trainee go through all eight steps on his/her own. Give immediate corrective feedback if necessary to make sure it is done correctly.

The second portion of the training segment is to prepare pancake batter. We will use the standardized recipe as our task breakdown (the actual content of the instruction).

1.f.2. Prepare Pancake Batter

Time: 6:10 AM

Place: Kitchen

Trainer: Breakfast Cook

Method: OTJ, Demonstration, and Practice

Duration: Ten minutes

Handout: Give the trainee a copy of standardized recipe.

Objective: Upon completion of the session, the trainee will be able to prepare pancake batter as per standards of GTI.

Yield: 50 4-inch pancakes

Ingredient	Amount	Procedure	Trainer's Directions
Flour Baking powder Baking soda Salt Sugar	2 lbs. 4 oz. 2 oz. 1.5 tsp. 1 tbs. 6 oz.	Place dry ingredients in mixer bowl. Mix on low speed until well blended, using flat beater.	"You have experience cooking and following recipes. We prepare one recipe of pancake batter fresh each morning. I will prepare this recipe showing you our techniques and where the ingredients and equipment are. Ask me any questions and tomorrow morning you will go ahead and make the pancakes yourself." [Gather all equipment & ingredients, read the recipe out loud, and follow it, explaining as you go.]

Ingredient	Amount	Procedure	Trainer's Directions
Eggs	6	In another bowl, beat eggs until light.	"We will dip out six eggs from the already broken eggs in the walk-in."
Buttermilk Vegetable Oil	7 C 1 C	Add milk and oil to eggs. Add to dry ingredients. Mix on low speed for thirty seconds. Use No. sixteen dipper to place batter on 350° griddle. Cook until surface of cake is full of bubbles. Turn pancakes and finish cooking till golden brown.	"Do not over-mix the batter." "Flip the pancakes only once."

Evaluation: On day number three of training, have the trainee prepare pancake batter on his/her own. Give immediate corrective feedback if necessary to make sure it is done correctly.

The muffin and French toast lesson plans would be constructed similarly. We use standardized recipes as the content and add the Trainer's Directions for demonstrations. By the time we are developing lesson plans, all task breakdowns should have been completed. [We addressed breakdowns in Chapter Six, although we did not actually do all the breakdowns for all the items on the job list for the cook position.]

2.a.4. Turn on oven

Time: 6:30 AM

Place: Kitchen

Trainer: Breakfast Cook

Method: OTJ and Demonstration

Duration: Two minutes

Objective: Upon completion of the session, the trainee will be able to turn on the oven as per standards of GTI.

Step	Procedure	Trainer's Directions
# 1	Adjust racks for muffin tins.	"We need to preheat the oven for muffins. We adjust the racks before it is heated so we do not lose heat adjusting them when we are ready to put the muffins in."
# 2	Close doors securely.	"Always keep the doors closed so we do not lose heat."
# 3	Power switch to "on"	
# 4	Fan switch to "cook"	"The fan must be on at all times when the oven is on so the oven does not burn up."
# 5	Temp knob to 375°	The convection oven bakes at a temperature about 25° cooler. And it bakes a little faster than you may be used to in a conventional oven. Always use long mitts so you do not burn the inside of your arms."
# 6	To turn off: Power switch to "off" Fan switch to "cool" Temp knob to "off"	"You turn it off the reverse way you turned it on—just flip both switches back to 'off' and 'cool,' and the temp to 'off.' Do not forget to turn off the fan."

Evaluation: Have the trainee start the oven on day number three. Check that it was done correctly.

Do You Really Need To Go Through All This To Start The Oven?

Turning on the oven is pretty simple. Even though training someone to start the oven can take just a minute or two, it is still important to develop a lesson plan. If we just say, "turn on the oven," and forget to go over all the steps, it is possible the oven might not be adequately preheated when we are ready to bake. The fan could have been left off and the oven subsequently damaged, or trainees might get burned if they forgot the mitts.

They would eventually learn the steps, but the lesson could be painful and/or expensive. We assure that the trainee does it right the first time, and every time, by showing new employees how to do it right.

OTJ training lesson plans are not terribly involved. An employee is already doing the job. The content is already there. Through lesson planning we are able to assure that all points that need stressing are stressed and not forgotten or skipped. We are able to assure that every trainee gets the same high-quality OTJ training no matter who the source is. We are not sure of that when we simply leave it up to chance, hoping that the employee doing the training will cover everything, cover it correctly, enthusiastically, and do it in a manner that the trainee will be able to understand.

The GTI: Off-The-Job Training Lesson Plans

Most training for the cook position is OTJ. There are a few items on the job list, however, that may best be taught in a format away from the actual job. Sanitation, storage and inventory, and the menu itself will be taught either in a classroom setting or in the storage areas. As with all lesson plans, we must begin with a task or job breakdown and an objective. Designing training that is away from the job involves more detail because the main activity—the trainer doing the job itself—is not occurring. We have to design the activities. We use the same lesson plan format, however.

We will design training for Storage and Inventory. In Chapter Eight we determined the training method, the trainer, where the training would be held, and we also scheduled the sessions.

Training Topic	Training Method	Trainer	Place Held
4) Storage and Inventory	Classroom, tour w/map, lecture and exercises, plus OTJ	Chef, 3 cooks	Storage areas and small conference room

Day #1: 7:00 AM to 3:30 PM

	Training Segment		Trainer	Where Held
7:20	4a, 4b	Tour plus storage and inventory	Chef	Storage areas

Day #2: 6:00 AM to 2:30 PM

Time	Training Segment		Trainer	Where Held
9:30	4a, 4b	Storage and Inventory	Chef	Storage areas

The Chef will be conducting a tour and instructing the cook trainee in storage and inventory practices. It was determined that storage should be addressed first because it would simplify OTJ training if the trainee was already familiar with storage areas and procedures. Sanitation training occurs immediately afterward because it is important that new employees use proper sanitation procedures right off the bat. Both storage and sanitation lessons will be conducted on days number and number two. Trainees will learn material more effectively if the sessions are brief, spaced over several days, and the material itself is repeated and practiced.

We will design a tour for the day number one session with a checklist so that it covers only necessary items. The checklist is a useful tool to help the trainer remember exactly what needs are to be covered and also to make sure the tour is conducted in the best possible order.

Tour Checklist

Time Clock

Locker Room and Personal Locker

Hand-washing

Dry Store Room

Walk-in

Freezer

Lesson Plan: Tour plus Storage and Inventory

Time: Day #1—7:20 AM

Place: Start in Dining Room after breakfast

Trainer: Chef

Method: Tour with demonstration and lecture

Duration: 1 hour

Objective: Upon completion of the tour, the trainee will be able to

1) Clock in

2) Wash hands

3) Locate items in various areas of the kitchen

4) Label and date

5) Keep running tally as per standards of GTI

Step	Procedure	Trainer's Directions
	Finish breakfast.	"We will be touring the kitchen in a minute. We are going to the employee locker room first so I can show you how to use the time clock." [Walk with trainee through the kitchen to the locker room and go to the time clock.]
#1	Time Clock: Find and remove your alphabetically ordered time card from rack.	"In order to get paid, you must clock in before your shift. I am going to show you how to clock in now, and later we will adjust the time so that you get paid for how long you have already been here. Find the time card with your name on it. They are kept in alphabetical order." [Point at the rack and have trainee pull his or her time card.]
#2	Push card into the horizontal slot until it clicks.	"Now you push the card all the way in. [Point to it.] Make sure the print side is up and your name goes in first. [Make sure the click sounds.] See?"
#3	Remove card and replace in rack.	Now put the card back in the rack where you found it. When your shift is done, clock out the same way: Find your card, push it into the slot, and replace your card. Do not forget to clock in and out every day because we need the completed card for payroll every other Friday."

(continues)

Step	Procedure	Trainer's Directions
		[Guide trainee into the locker room.] "This locker is for your use. Keep the key in your pocket and always lock up your stuff. We do not want to tempt anyone to steal anything."
		When you arrive for your shift, you will stow your belongings in this locker and then clock in. Then you enter the kitchen through this door." [Guide trainee through door and go to the hand-washing sink.]
		"Your first stop is always the hand-washing sink where you will thoroughly wash your hands." [Point to the hand-washing poster above the sink and demonstrate the technique shown on the poster by doing and explaining each step.]
1	Hand-washing: Use water as hot as the hands can comfortably stand.	
2	Moisten hands, soap thoroughly, and lather to elbow.	
3	Scrub thoroughly, using brush for nails.	
4	Rub hands together, using friction for twenty seconds.	
5	Rinse thoroughly under running water.	
6	Dry hands, using paper towel over the hand sink.	"Do not dry your hands on your apron or your towel. If you touch anything that might contaminate your hands, wash them again using this procedure. Most food-borne

Step	Procedure	Trainer's Directions
		illnesses come from contamination and hands cause the most problems. Now, wash your hands using the steps I just demonstrated." [Watch and give any corrective or positive feedback necessary to be sure trainee uses proper hand-washing techniques.]
	Dry Store Room	[Guide trainee to the dry store room while explaining:] "Some of the ingredients the cooks use all the time are kept at the cook's station. All other ingredients are either stored in the dry store room, the walk-in, or the freezer. This is our dry store room where we stock all ingredients that are kept at room temperature. The store room is kept locked at all times. You and the other cooks each have a key and are responsible for the contents of all the storage areas in the kitchen."
1	Ingredient locations	[Guide trainee around store room, pointing out where everything is located. Explain the rationale.] "The spices are ordered by type. See, here are all the baking spices, here are the seeds, here are herbs, here are hot spices, and so on. Nothing is directly placed on the floor, and we try to keep adequate space between things and the walls so we can dust and clean easily. All the baking supplies are here [point to area] and canned goods are here, and so forth.
2	FIFO	"We use First-In-First-Out and always put the new in back of the old. As we put new items away, we use this marker [point to the

(continues)

Step	Procedure	Trainer's Directions
2		marker] and record a date on the item. Any time you see an item in any of the storage areas that does not look right (starting to rot, etc.) you must notify me or Kate (Sous Chef), and we will decide what to do with the item. Our rule is, "When in doubt, throw it out." We do not want to have to throw out any food because of careless management, though, as that increases our food cost and reduces profit. So, we are very careful about keeping track of all food and using it in a timely way."
3	Wrap, Label and Date	"Again, we label and date everything in all our storage areas to make sure we know what things are and how old they are. There are rolls of masking tape and markers in this box here, and at several different locations throughout the kitchen." [Point to them in the storage areas and every place in the kitchen as you walk through.] "Nothing is ever to be put in any of the storage areas or units without label and dating."
4	Inventory Records	We keep a running tally of everything in our inventory. When you take anything from any of the storage areas, you are to note it on the inventory tally sheet attached beneath the item's storage place." [Point out and explain the last notation on several of the tally sheets.]
a	Running tally—mark off anything you remove from storage areas on tally sheet.	
b	At the end of the evening shift, take physical inventory of expensive items and compare with tally.	"At the end of the evening shift, the cooks take a physical inventory of expensive items such as meats, cheeses, and desserts ... and they compare the physical count with the tally. The cook on duty will show you how this is done when you close on the fourth and fifth days of training."

Step	Procedure	Trainer's Directions
c	Physical inventory at the end of every month.	"At the end of each month, we count every item in all the storage areas. You will go through inventory at that time. It is very similar to closing inventory and you won't find it difficult. We will walk you through it."
	Walk-in Refrigerator	"Now let us go over to the walk-in." [Guide trainee into the refrigerator.] "Keep the door shut at all times. Do not worry about being locked in, as that is impossible. [Show trainee the inner locking mechanism.] Always remember to turn off the light when you leave. The light gives off heat and uses energy . . . and, obviously, we do not want any of the cold air escaping."
1	Walk-in Temperature	"The walk-in should always remain at 40° or below. Make a point of always checking the thermometer. Tell me or Kate (Sous Chef) immediately if the temperature is ever over 40°."
2 3 4 5	Ingredient Location FIFO Label & Date Inventory	[Guide the trainee through the walk-in just like the storeroom. Explain ingredient location, FIFO, Label and Dating, and inventory tally. Go over inventory for the walk-in. It is the same as for the storeroom above.]
	Freezer	"Let us go into the freezer now. Here is a jacket to wear if you are spending more than a few minutes inside." [Show trainee where jacket is kept and have him or her put it on.]
1	Freezer Temperature	"Check the thermometer all the time and make sure the freezer

(continues)

Step	Procedure	Trainer's Directions
		stays at 0° or below. Tell me or Kate (Sous Chef) if it is ever above 0°. Again, turn off the light when you leave the freezer because it wastes energy and gives off heat. Close but do not seal the door when you are in the freezer. We do not want to let in any heat."
2 3 4 5	Ingredient Location FIFO Label & Date Inventory	[Take trainee through the freezer just like the storeroom and the walk-in. Explain ingredient location, FIFO, Label and Dating, and inventory tally, plus inventory for the freezer. It is the same as for the storeroom and walk-in.]

Practice: The trainee will be doing OTJ training and the trainer will review FIFO, label and dating, and inventory within the context of the job. The day number two session on Storage and Inventory will include some storage and inventory exercises to assure that the trainee knows how to do all things taught in the previous session.

A lesson plan for the day two session would also need to be developed. It is time consuming to put together good lesson plans. If you were only going to train one person, it would not be worth the effort. However, most operations today are training people with regularity. Having lesson plans means that we have excellent training every time with no preparation.

CONCLUSION

Designing training is not difficult. It is tedious! The work is not for everyone. A good designer has the ability to conceptualize the big picture. Break it into its smallest possible parts and apply instructional design technology such as learning principles and methods. No detail is too small for an instructional designer.

Our task is to assure that every trainee masters the material, though. That is impossible if our training is inconsistent and inconclusive. We do not want to leave anything up to chance. If one of the employees we are training grasps the material immediately, we can move through it quickly without repetition. We do not, however, assume that any employee knows the material and, therefore, skip over it. Assumptions mean we could be wrong. We certainly do not want to find out from a customer that our assumption was wrong. To that end, we include all details necessary to properly do the job for the facility for which we are designing training. We assure that every employee masters the training and is not practicing on customers.

CHAPTER THOUGHT QUESTIONS

1. Define lesson plans and discuss why all instruction must have one. Be sure to include all the benefits of having lesson plans.

2. In task analysis, we break down the duty into sequential steps and include procedures and performance standards. What is the difference between a lesson plan and a completed task analysis? Describe the relationship between the two.

3. Describe in detail the components of a training plan in Chapter Eight. Which of the parts are used in the lesson plan? How are they used? Where are they in the lesson plan?

4. When we write lesson plans, we use procedures from the task analysis and structure from the training plan. What do we actually write that is new when we develop the lesson plan?

5. Once we are ready to begin writing lesson plans, where do we start? Describe in detail the process for writing lesson plans.

6. Describe the similarities and differences between lesson plans for on-the-job training and off-the-job training.

7. Which lesson plans are more involved to write—on-the-job or off-the-job training? Why?

8. Most items on a job list for hospitality line positions are suitable for OTJ training. Some duties or steps of duties, however, might best be taught in classroom settings. List a few examples of duties that might best be taught in classroom settings.

9. Is it necessary to develop lesson plans for training someone if you are only going to train one person for that position once? No one would ever be hired for that position again. Explain your answer.

10. Discuss objectives—where they fit in lesson plans, where the objectives came from, what the purpose of objectives are, and why they are necessary in lesson plans.

10 Group Training and Team-building

Objectives

Most training we do is with individuals hired to replace other employees. Sometimes we find that we must train a group of new employees, though, such as in an opening, or we must re-train a group of employees if something changes in the business. The training design process, however, is the same for both group and individual training.

The purpose of this chapter is to demonstrate the training design process in a group training situation. Upon completion of Chapter Ten, the student should be able to

- List and describe the differences and similarities between group and individual training design and implementation.

- Describe group dynamics and explain how teams are built and maintained in a work environment.

- Discuss employee diversity and differences in learning styles. Describe teaching methods that may be effective in accommodating these differences.

- Design a training segment for a group training session.

Group Training

We are very familiar with classes in school. Good teachers generally come to class prepared with planned activities that make sense to us. They may have lecture notes, overheads, perhaps a quiz, activity, or an assignment. The lesson is planned and all activities and materials are designed to attain the particular lesson's objective. Instructional and training design are the same process. A lesson on writing behavioral objectives in a college course on *Training Design for the Hospitality Industry* is developed the same as any group training.

The objective of the lesson would be: "Upon completion of the lesson, students should be able to write behavioral objectives for a segment of training for any line position in the hospitality industry." This objective is a behavioral objective because the students are expected to be able to *do* something after the lesson, not just know or understand. That means we must design instruction that will result in students actually writing behavioral objectives.

This in-class lesson is similar to group training because there are more than one or two students in the class, and it is similar to training because we are teaching them to do something that could be considered vocational (to design training for their future companies). **Group training** is training more than one employee at the same time to do the same task and may also be done in a classroom rather than OTJ. We may be more familiar with formal group training in school rather than in work settings, so we will first look at planning a lesson to accompany a reading from this textbook and then design a group training lesson for GTI.

Instructional Design

Let's revisit the training design model.

Step #1	#2	#3	#4	#5	#6	#7
Needs Assessment	Training Plan	Lesson Plans	Trainer Training	Training Implementation	Training Evaluation	Coaching and Counseling

A course in training design for the hospitality industry is most likely being taught because someone determined there was a need for a course of this nature. The lesson on behavioral objectives is one of many and is taught on the particular day because of its position in the training plan. We are assuming steps one and two were already done, so now we are ready to develop the lesson plan for teaching students to write objectives.

A one-hour lesson on writing behavioral objectives is scheduled in the normal classroom reserved for the course, and we are anticipating approximately twenty students. The participants are primarily nineteen-year-old students in a university hospitality management program who have at least some experience in the hospitality industry. Our task is to determine the content to be taught and how best to teach it. The basis of the content exists in Chapter Eight of the textbook where behavioral objectives are covered. That section will be the assigned reading for the lesson.

The objective, "Upon completion of the lesson, students should be able to write behavioral objectives for a segment of training for any line position in the hospitality industry," remains our focus for lesson planning. As designers, we might begin by reading the text material covering writing behavioral objectives. If all students in the class will be able to meet the objective by simply reading the textbook material, our lesson plan could be to assign the reading and then give a quiz where they have to write a behavioral objective.

Training Methods

Unlike education, everyone being trained *must* meet the objective. It's unlikely that all of the students would be able to write behavioral objectives just by reading the chapter, so we will need to design some activities to assure this. Lectures, demonstrations, role-plays, and simulations (as described in Chapter Seven) may be appropriate group training method choices for most hospitality line positions. The main difference in using these methods with groups, rather than individuals, is making sure that everyone in the group can see, hear, practice, and understand.

For the lesson on how to write behavioral objectives, it might be useful for the instructor to review and perhaps expand on the chapter material and provide some examples of behavioral objectives. Under the direction of the instructor, the class as a whole could devise behavioral objectives for various training situations they might be familiar with. Then students could work in pairs devising behavioral objectives for more situations, and, finally, they could create some individually. Each situation and behavioral objective could be discussed so that all students eventually are writing the same objective. Their ability to write behavioral objectives could be tested with yet another training situation for which they would have to demonstrate this skill.

The objective of the lesson determined the methods (review and practice with immediate corrective feedback) and also determined the test (writing a behavioral objective). A lesson plan (utilizing a standard format that includes detailed instructions for delivering the content and activities and copies of handouts, overheads, example objectives, practice training situations and keys, behavioral tests, etc.) is then constructed.

The design process is the same for all classes in school, for individual training, and for group training. We have experienced many different classes in school from finger painting in kindergarten to perhaps college physics or biology. The classes and content and methods of instruction may have been very different. The design process, however, remains the same. The main difference between individual and group training is that the former can be tailored to the individual's learning style and training needs, whereas group training must address various learning styles and training needs.

Training Diverse Employees

Training is designed to meet the learning needs of most trainees. Not everyone learns in the same way, though, or at the same speed. Chapter One described the diversity of the workforce. When designing lessons for group training situations in the hospitality industry, it is very likely that the composition of groups to be trained will be diverse. **Diversity** is all the human characteristics that make us different from each other. It is essential to provide training content and activities that will be effective for trainees with different backgrounds and learning styles.

As people, we are more alike than different. Disabilities, gender, learning styles, language, age, race, ethnicity, etc., are differences that can influence the way we think and perceive others. Beneath these obvious differences, however, are the same human emotions. We all are familiar with love, anger, fear, joy, hurt, and excitement. We all care about our children and desire successful lives. Sometimes life situations block healthy responses, but all humans have the capacity for the same emotions. If we are aware of differences between us (and how these differences affect learning), we can design training that is received by individuals without differences getting in the way.

Some of us prefer learning by reading or attending a lecture. Others find working on a project more effective. Some people need to see the "big picture" before getting into details, while others prefer dealing with specifics. Some people are very theoretical while others want to do something active.

Some people prefer working alone while others like to work in groups. A good match between learning styles and training methods can result in more effective and efficient instruction. A "hands-on" type may not profit from a lecture. A "big-picture" person may be very frustrated by instruction that only eventually puts all the little pieces together to result in the whole.

Group training is designed for the typical worker but can be made more effective if we include a variety of methods to allow for the learning style preferences of our trainees. The training designer and the trainer have their own learning style preferences, too. We want to make sure that we are not designing training for just the way we like to learn, without taking into consideration the various learning styles of our target market. We might want to provide both the "big picture" for those trainees that need it and the sequential building detail for those who need that. We can require certain amounts of individual work but then require group work also. We can relate theory to actual concrete experience. One of the adult learning principles in Chapter Seven says that adults learn best when they have received the material in several different ways. In short, by providing for individual learning style preferences . . . we are going to end up with better instruction.

Training Disabled Employees

Many people with disabilities can have successful hospitality careers. It has been suggested that we are all disabled—it's just a matter of degree. Alcoholism, addiction to drugs, shopping, food, relationships, gambling, obsessive-compulsive behavior, etc., are examples of disabilities that may not be noticeable but can affect the way we think or behave.

Our task as managers is not to heal our employees, but to figure out how to get them all functioning to standards. If we eliminate or do not hire people with problems, we will have very few employees. We hire people with disabilities because we need them, and also because it is illegal to not hire them. The same rules apply for hiring people with disabilities, though. They must be willing and able to do the job (with reasonable accommodation), and then must be trained to do the job.

Standards do not change for disabled employees. Our training, however, must be designed to accommodate the disabilities so that every trainee masters the material. The disability does not define the employee; rather, it is just one characteristic that must be dealt with. People with disabilities have personalities, desires, likes and dislikes that may have nothing to do with being disabled. If a blind person is part of our group training session, we will have to design materials that can be utilized by the blind person also. All visual materials would need to be described verbally. Similarly, hearing disabled employees would need verbal materials in written form. If we are unsure what accommodations disabled people might need, we can ask them for specifics.

Employees with obvious physical disabilities (such as crutches or confinement to a wheel chair) may have difficulties with physical barriers, could easily tire, or could be late due to transportation problems. Some flexibility will be necessary. Not all disabilities are physically obvious. Learning disabilities might not be readily identifiable and could require additional time and instruction delivered in a variety of ways. Chronic disabilities such as diabetes, AIDS, cardiac conditions, etc., can affect attention span, stamina, and performance consistency. Again, some flexibility will be necessary.

If the people we hire are willing and able to do the job, we can design training materials that are appropriate for their particular disability. We will design training materials for the typical employee, but can then modify the materials for specific needs of the trainees. Providing a variety of methods to meet the diverse learning needs of all our employees will result in better training for everyone.

Group Dynamics and Team-building

We can begin with a group of employees needing to be trained. Teaching them necessary job skills through the use of well-designed training materials may be the easier part. Turning the group into a team (prepared to work together to meet guests' needs) requires special training and management skills. A **team** is a group that works together to meet a common goal. Groups can form without planning, but teams are planned, built, and developed, and their members are often selected for specialized skills.

Teams are usually more effective than individuals working alone. The statement, "That's not on my job description," is not an indication of team effort. Most of us are familiar with sports teams and understand that team members cannot all be individual stars. They must work together as one team to get the ball in the basket or across the goal line. Team members must communicate in order to work together. The task of the manager or trainer is to provide the goal, the incentive, and to facilitate communication.

Personal ambitions and desires that are not shared by the rest of the team must be subordinated for the good of the cause. Managers or trainers who are attuned to the needs of the employees may provide reasons that align employee needs with meeting the team's goal. For instance, employees who desire promotions or more pay can come to see the team's goal as a vehicle to where they want to be. Competition between team members can lead to conflict and reduce cooperation and may be avoided by open communication of team member's individual responsibilities. Members of sports teams have assigned positions with specific roles and responsibilities.

Each member of the team must do his or her part (and do it well) or the whole team suffers. Conflict can result when a team member is misbehaving or slacking off. It is the responsibility of the manager or trainer to find out what is going on with the individual and figure out how to resolve the problem. Ordering an employee to "Get with the program" is as ineffective as ignoring the problem altogether. Only communication can help employees to understand their common interest in the team effort.

Team-building Strategies

Expecting employees to act as a team requires them to be more than just order takers. We are asking them to think and make decisions within the context of a goal. To enable employees to work at this higher thinking level, we must allow them participation in the planning and decision-making process for the team. They must be given the direction and information necessary to determine how to move toward the goal in a feasible, efficient, and acceptable way. Team members can meet, discuss, and decide strategies for attaining the goal with the manager or trainer acting as facilitator—keeping the team on track.

Ongoing positive open communication fosters involvement within the team. Team members who care about each other tend to work together better. The manager or trainer must be a member of the team—a member with an assigned position with a specific role and responsibility, that of facilitator, communicator, and director. Each member of the team is equally important. Each team member has specific responsibilities that must be met for the team to be successful. Team members can work together beautifully for a long period of time and then suddenly have problems become apparent. Just like happily married couples can occasionally have misunderstandings or bad days, so too can teams. It is the manager or trainer that must redirect the negative energies back to productivity.

Team meetings are necessary to keep the communication flow open and to assure that everyone stays informed. Most of us have been to long, boring, inconvenient, unproductive, and pointless employee meetings.

Careful planning must precede the meeting to assure there is indeed a point to it and that employees leave feeling that the exercise was useful. Meetings should be convenient for employees, they should be on company time, and they should be short. Meetings should allow for the opinions of employees to be voiced and listened to with respect. Most of all, meetings should be productive. It is the responsibility of the person conducting the meeting to keep the direction and focus positive. Complaints can be turned into opportunities to brainstorm solutions, which in turn can have a team-building effect.

Group Training Design for GTI

These days, success in the hospitality industry is all about *teamwork*. Teams do not just happen, they are built. We have a diverse work force, and almost any group training in our business will involve diversity. No matter what the primary objective of the group training session may be, team-building is almost always a secondary objective. Our task is to design training for a diverse group, incorporating team-building, so the behavioral training objective is met and the trained group becomes more of a team.

Jim, General Manager of GTI, has decided to implement an employee incentive program. He initially brought up the concept at a previous managers' meeting where the idea was favorably received. Kelly, the Assistant General Manager, then worked with him to flesh out a program to reward employee excellence. The management staff will need to be trained to use this program, and staff will need to be notified. Ergo, group training and an employee meeting plan become necessary.

Kelly has been given the responsibility for creating both the training and the employee meeting. Chapter Eleven describes how to train the trainer. All managers and OTJ trainers were put through train-the-trainer instruction. Kelly also took a training design course so she would be able to design any additional training that might become necessary once the consultants finished the initial training design for all positions at GTI.

The Training Design Model gave Kelly a pattern to follow in preparing training documents that would result in successful utilization of the incentive program. Kelly and Jim agreed it was necessary to train managers so they would know how to reward employee excellence. It is a simple program, and Kelly figured she could adequately train the managers in about an hour. They also determined that training could take place during the regularly scheduled managers' meeting. Steps one and two (Needs

Assessment and Training Plan) are far more involved when we are looking at problems with existing procedures instead of something new or when the training is comprehensive.

The five managers to be trained are between the ages of twenty-two and forty. They have all been at GTI for at least two years and work well as a team. Upon completion of training, managers will be able to

1. Explain the advantages and workings of the new employee incentive program.

2. Reward employee excellence appropriately and fairly as per the incentive program.

A lecture with discussion afterward will be conducted to meet the first objective. Examples in the form of brief case studies, simulations, and work sheets will be utilized to meet the second. A handout with instructions and expectations will be distributed to managers and a follow-up session will be held after the first month of implementation to evaluate and modify if necessary.

Task Analysis

Any time we design instruction or training, we have to break the objective into steps or elements the trainee must be taught. If we skip this tedious step, we could design training that is incomplete or incorrect.

Go back and consider the objective.

For number one of the objective, we first have to identify the advantages and how the program works. We cannot teach managers to explain the advantages and workings if we do not know specifically what they are. Going through this process will also help clarify the program and pinpoint any inherent problems. Kelly lists what she thinks are advantages of the program and what GTI hopes to gain from implementation. She asks Jim to make his own list and then compares the two. She asks questions such as: Is each advantage and gain on the list realistic? Can we really get this gain from the program?

Kelly's Advantages and Gains:

a) Recognition of excellent work makes employees feel appreciated.

b) Employees will be motivated to do excellent work in order to receive recognition and rewards.

c) Managers may be more appreciated by employees because they are paying more positive attention to employees' performance.

d) Morale and job satisfaction will increase.

e) Customer satisfaction will increase.

Jim's list turned out to be similar. While comparing them, though, Kelly realized that the lists were comprised of assumptions. They assume employees will feel appreciated and will work for the recognition and rewards—they do not know for sure. If employees do not feel appreciated or want to work for recognition and rewards, is there any point in going forward with the program? They put a list of rewards together. If employees do indeed respond to rewards, are these the right rewards? After talking it over with Jim, Kelly decided to put together a focus group of employees to get their reaction to the program and any input that might make it a better match.

Employees selected from the various departments were known to be popular and informal leaders. They thought the program sounded great. They liked the rewards and thought it was good that they could save up certificates like coupons and redeem bigger prizes. They agreed that they liked it when their good work was recognized and said they tended to work better for managers who appreciated their effort. They thought employees would be motivated by the program. They were, however, concerned that some managers might be miserly with certificates, give them only to their own employees, and/or not notice everyone's work equitably. Their concerns would have to be addressed in the training.

Kelly and Jim decided they did not wish to measure the effect of the program on employee morale, satisfaction, and customer satisfaction. They were satisfied with their assumption that the program would have a beneficial effect and were reasonably certain that it would, at least, not have a negative effect on employees and customers. Had the employees been negative and closed to the Employee Excellence Incentive Program, it would have been best to rethink the entire idea. Through the focus group, Kelly found that items (a) and (b) on the list of advantages and gains were affirmed, and that items (c), (d), and (e) were intuitively probable. They also came to understand possible problems in implementation that could have a negative effect on employees.

The written Employee Excellence Incentive Program serves as a description of the program.

The GTI Employee Excellence Incentive Program

Employees who exceed the standards or who go above and beyond the expectations of GTI can be rewarded on the spot, by any manager, with a certificate indicating the noted excellence. The certificates can be redeemed for small prizes such as free dinners or collected and exchanged for larger prizes like paid days off, etc. (See prize list posted in the employee break room.)

The second part of number one of the objective is that managers should also be able to explain how the program works. To explain how it actually works is to focus on number two in the objective: "Reward employee excellence appropriately and fairly as per the incentive program." Kelly must do task analysis to determine the steps for awarding certificates, and she will use a modified version of task analysis from Chapter Six.

Duty: Award Certificates for Excellence

Step	Procedure	Performance Standard	Need To Do
1	Managers are to carry blank certificates and a pen at all times.	• Carry at least five certificates and a working pen.	Develop certificate.
2	Managers who notice any employee exceeding standards should give the employee a filled-out certificate on-the-spot if possible.	• Managers should generally focus on employees in their own departments. • Managers should never give out certificates for unexceptional performance; however, it would be reasonable for a manager to give out one per ten workers per week. • No employee should receive more than one certificate for the same performance behavior within a month.	Develop "exceeding standards" guidelines. Develop record-keeping procedures and forms.

(continues)

Duty: Award Certificates for Excellence *(cont.)*

Step	Procedure	Performance Standard	Need To Do
3	[Do task analysis for filling out the form—not included here.]	[Not included but would need to be if this was real!]	

Task analysis would also need to be done for redeeming certificates for both employees and those who do the redeeming. This task analysis would be content for the portion of the employees' meeting where the new Employee Excellence Incentive Program is announced and for training the employees who redeem certificates for rewards.

Lesson Plan

Step number three in the model is to develop the lesson plan. Kelly has already determined the objectives, target market, methods, when and where the training will take place, and the trainer. The hidden objectives for this training are to encourage enthusiastic acceptance of the program by managers and to nurture team spirit. Getting employee reactions and input prior to planning and implementation opens the program to acceptance.

Kelly has identified all steps that managers must go through. She will develop the guidelines and forms identified in *Need To Do*, and, once those are done, she will write the lesson plans (as in Chapter Nine) to share content with the managers in such a way as to meet training objectives. Writing lesson plans for individual or group training is the same. We must, however, make sure that everyone in the group can see, hear, and understand the material. We will build those checks into the lesson plan.

Lesson Plan—Employee Excellence Incentive Program

Time: At the regularly scheduled Managers' Meeting

Place: Jim's office conference area

Trainer: Kelly

Method: Lecture with discussion, brief case studies, simulation, and worksheets

Duration: One hour

Objective: Upon completion of training, managers will be able to

1. Explain the advantages and how the new employee incentive program works.

2. Reward employee excellence appropriately and fairly as per the incentive program.

Step	Procedure	Trainer's Directions
1	Introduction and welcome	[Everyone should be sitting around the table.] **Jim**: "You all remember the discussion we had at the last meeting about the employee incentive program idea I had. Your reaction was favorable and thoughtful. Since then, Kelly and I have worked out the details incorporating your input and also employee input, so we are ready to go with it. I have asked Kelly to train us this morning so we all know how to do it." **Kelly**: "I think we have a really nice little program here that is going to be good for all of us. I am going to take about thirty minutes to show you how to use it."
2	Describe the Program. **The GTI Employee Excellence Incentive Program** Employees who exceed standards or who go above and beyond the expectations of GTI can be rewarded on the spot, by any manager, with a certificate indicating the noted excellence. The certificates may be redeemed for small prizes such as free dinners or may be collected and exchanged for larger prizes like paid days off, etc. (See prize list posted in the employee break room.)	"I am giving you a handout that describes the new Employee Excellence Incentive Program." [Hand out the EEIP info sheet. (This sheet is not included here, but it would have to be if this was real!) Read the description out loud.] "You will notice the description is pretty much the one we worked out in our discussion at the last meeting." [Pointing out the use of the managers' input helps acceptance.] "We will go over the rest of the info sheet in the next few minutes."

(continues)

Step	Procedure	Trainer's Directions
3	Describe the Advantages and Gains of the Program: a. Recognition of excellent work makes employees feel appreciated. b. Employees will be motivated to do excellent work in order to receive recognition and rewards. c. Managers may be more appreciated by employees because they are paying more positive attention to employees' performance. d. Morale and job satisfaction will increase. e. Customer satisfaction will increase.	"John and I met with the employees you identified as informal leaders in your departments, and they thought the incentive program sounded really good." [Employee and manager involvement help the acceptance.] "Now, this program is going to cost us some money . . . and it is going to take time. We are, of course, hoping it will be beneficial. Do you think it will?" [Guide a discussion about how to bring out all the advantages and gains. Ask questions such as: Do you think the employees will like it? Will they work for the rewards? Is this good?" Will this be good for you as managers? How? What about morale and job satisfaction? Could this have an effect on our customers? What might it be? Make sure everyone is contributing—call the managers by name and, if one has not said much, ask: "What do you think, Paul?"] "You will notice on your info sheet that we have listed advantages for employees and also for GTI. We want our employees to be enthusiastic about this program and these statements are worded in ways that may sound good to them. [Read over the statement (not included here, but it would have to be if this was real!) and get manager's input on them and reword or change them if necessary.]
4	How to Award Certificates for Employee Excellence 1. Managers are to carry blank certificates and a pen at all times.	"Here are the Certificates." [Pass them out to all the managers.] (The instruction would continue here, utilizing the chosen methods and materials, none of which have been designed for this example.)

Step	Procedure	Trainer's Directions
	2. Managers who notice any employee exceeding standards should give the worker a filled-out certificate on the spot if possible.	
	3. [How to fill out the form content comes from task analysis which was not completed for this example.]	

CONCLUSION

The first part of the uncompleted lesson plan for training managers—how to implement the EEIP—was included to serve as an example for designing group training. The design process is exactly the same as for individual training. It is a very time-consuming process but assures comprehensive training, which will greatly increase the effectiveness and success of the program's implementation.

To design good training, we must precisely identify the results we wish to realize. We must write behavioral objectives. Everything follows from these objectives. Utilizing the Training Design Model gives us a step-by-step approach for a process that is essentially common sense.

KEY WORDS

Group Training   Team

Diversity

CHAPTER THOUGHT QUESTIONS

1. Identify several training situations, in your experience, where group training might be necessary.
2. Discuss the design process similarities between individual training and group training. Describe the differences.

3. List and describe training methods that may be appropriate for group training. Are they different methods than we might use for individual training?

4. List and describe the differences in people that make for diversity.

5. Why must we accommodate diversity in our trainees rather than expect everyone to be like us?

6. List and describe accommodations that we might make to enable diverse trainees to successfully complete the training.

7. Discuss the importance of team-building in the workplace. Do we need to have teams?

8. List and describe some team-building strategies.

9. List and describe the steps in the Training Design Model. Why are they important and why do we use the model?

10. In the partial Lesson Plan example for the Employee Excellence Incentive Program, identify directions that were designed to encourage teamwork and employee acceptance of the program and training.

REFERENCES

Davis, B. G. (2001). *Tools for Teaching.* California: Jossey-Bass.

11 | *Train-the-Trainer*

OBJECTIVES

Not everyone can be a good teacher. Some people have it in them to be good teachers, but start slowly and are not very good at first. To wit, seasoned teachers are usually better than new ones. Most of us improve with practice. Teaching someone to do a job takes entirely different skills than just doing the job. Most people selected by management to train new employees have the job skills down. Often, however, they have not been shown how to train and do not have the skills necessary for teaching someone else how to do the job. Merely being good at specific jobs like waiter, cook, or front desk does not qualify one for trainer responsibilities.

The purpose of this chapter is to review and practice instructional design by designing instruction to train the trainer. This instruction can be modified to use in any hospitality operation to train line workers to be trainers.

Upon completion of Chapter Eleven, the student should be able to

- Discuss the importance of train-the-trainer instruction.
- Describe the characteristics necessary to be a successful trainer.
- Design or modify instruction to train-the-trainer.

Train-the-Trainer Instruction

As professionals we want to take as much guesswork and risk out of our management as possible. Giving responsibilities to untrained trainers increases the chance that new employees may not be taught properly, and, as a result, will not be able to meet customer standards. Even if there are professionally designed training documents, untrained trainers might not know how to use them or may not even bother. When we go to the effort and expense to design training, we then must train the people who are going to deliver the material to new employees. Otherwise, we are wasting resources, and our new employees may not be competent before taking the floor.

Some of us may intuitively know the principles of learning and how to get people to do what we want them to do. While some of us are naturally great communicators (good listeners, tuned in to the feelings of those around us), the greater majority of people could probably use some work on communication skills. The over 50 percent divorce rate is an indication of less than highly developed communication skills in our country. Those "natural" teachers will also benefit from instruction in basic training or teaching principles and methods. Great teachers practice and hone their skills. They go to workshops, retreats, read articles about teaching, and keep their approach to education fresh.

Most of us understand the necessity of training employees to do their jobs. We know that some methods are better than others. We may have personally experienced excellent comprehensive training for a position in one hospitality organization, then changed jobs and experienced a much less effective system. If we expect an employee to train other employees, it stands to reason that we should train the employee to be able to effectively do his or her new job duties. We train cooks. We train servers. We train front desk agents. We train housekeepers. We must also train trainers.

Trainer Characteristics

In Chapter Two, we described some of the characteristics trainers need. As with all jobs, we need to make sure we have good matches between person and position. Not everyone can be a good server. Not everyone is good with the general public. Not everyone can be an accountant. Even if we are forced to take jobs or receive certain training, we may not be successful or happy if it is not a good match (i.e., our own characteristics match those necessary for the position).

A great cook may be asked to train a new cook. To be a great cook requires expertise, the ability to do many things simultaneously, a sense of timing, and the ability to work fast in a highly stressful atmosphere. It does not require exceptional communication skills or the ability to explain and demonstrate things clearly and patiently. On the other hand, a trainer need not be a great cook to teach other cooks to be great cooks . . . so long as the other people have the characteristics it takes to be great cooks. A master chef, however, will not necessarily make a great trainer.

Obviously, a trainer needs a certain level of subject matter expertise. It would be difficult for you to teach someone to cook without any cooking skills of your own. But, more than subject matter expertise, a trainer needs to be able to patiently, sequentially, and clearly explain a process. A trainer needs to be able to be attuned to the trainee—to know whether or not the trainee is following and understanding the material—and to be able to modify the training to better meet the needs of the trainee. The trainer needs to understand and incorporate the principles of learning while providing an atmosphere conducive to learning.

Not everyone wants the additional responsibility of training. We should not force employees to train other employees. Instead, we should determine who wants to train and select trainers who have the required characteristics from that group. To simply add training responsibilities to an existing job can be motivating for some high-achiever type employees. It can, however, also have the effect of causing a feeling of resentment. An employee may feel overworked and under-appreciated—working harder than others in the same position but for the same pay. We may want to consider additional pay for the additional responsibilities of training (i.e., "trainer's pay"), or, perhaps, allowing employees to be freed from some of their regular job responsibilities while training new workers. Either way, training means additional expenses.

Once we have selected someone who wants to train other employees (who possesses the required communication skills, is attuned to other people, is flexible, patient, and can explain things clearly), we can then teach this person motivation theory, learning principles, teaching methods, and how to use and perhaps design lesson plans.

Design Train-the-Trainer Instruction

We use the same training design model to design trainer training.

Step #1	#2	#3	#4	#5	#6	#7
Needs Assessment	Training Plan	Lesson Plans	Trainer Training	Training Implementation	Training Evaluation	Coaching and Counseling

We begin with needs assessment. We ask ourselves questions like: Who is the trainer and what do they do? What does the trainer have to know to be able to do it? How and where do we find this information? We use the needs assessment tools—job lists and job or task breakdowns, and then we write objectives and come up with a training plan. Lesson plans are then devised to result in attainment of the objectives. So, we go back to Chapter Three and begin.

GTI: Train-the-Trainer Needs Assessment

We know we need to design training for the trainer because we do not have any. We have already collected data on the organization mission and philosophy and the extent of management commitment to training. We know about space and time availability and organizational and individual needs. We need to find out about the position needs.

Position needs (from Chapter Three):
- Obtain a copy of the organizational chart.
- What are the duties and responsibilities of each of the positions? (Job descriptions)
- What are the qualifications necessary for each of the positions? (Job specifications)
- What type of training is necessary for each of the positions?
- Task Analysis

We already have a copy of the organizational chart. We are only interested at this point in the position of trainer. We will need a job description and job specification for trainer. In hospitality operations, much of our training will be OTJ. As a result, many of our trainers will be workers doing the job. Much of the same training could probably be given to all the trainers in all departments at GTI.

Training differs from education in many ways. We need only train people for what they actually have to do. We do not need to bother with background, history, or any explanations that do not have a direct effect on the job. In the kitchen, the Chef, Sous Chef, and probably representatives from all the line positions will be actively involved in training. It is likely, however, that some of the line workers (such as the dish person) will have fairly small training demands. It may not be necessary to teach this person everything there is to know about training. He or she may only need to be trained to use the training lesson plan. The Chef and the other department heads, on the other hand, will probably need to have a comprehensive understanding of all training principles and methods. They will not only be taught how to deliver the training, but also be expected to design training themselves.

We might want to design comprehensive train-the-trainer instruction where portions could be used to train those trainers whose training needs are less. We could pull out the portion on "how to do a demonstration according to a lesson plan" to train a dishwasher to train another dishwasher, and so forth. Part of the comprehensive training instruction might include how to pull out portions from the comprehensive instruction and modify them specifically for the lesser needs of some departmental employees who will be training others.

Training Needs

We have decided to design a comprehensive train-the-trainer program for the management team at GTI. The Executive Chef, Executive Housekeeper, Front Desk Manager, and the Dining Room Manager, plus the Assistant General Manager and Sous Chef will all receive instruction. The GM will also sit in on all these sessions. They will all be taught to use specific segments of the comprehensive training to show their own staff members how to train.

We need a job list in order to begin the design process. There is, however, no employee or manager who can show or tell us what the trainer to be trained needs to know. We are, after all, designing training for a position that, up to now, has not existed. As for new operations, we must obtain the information from experts or other operations that have similar training programs. In the case of GTI, the information will come from the expert consultants (us) who were contracted to design the training.

Define the Trainees

Training will be designed for the seven members of GTI's management team. Three have bachelor degrees, one has an associate degree, and two have high school diplomas. They all have good reading and communication skills, and have been successfully managing their departments or areas. Portions of the training materials will be modified by managers for training selected line workers to train (OTJ Trainers).

Job Specification: OTJ Trainers

1) Must be able to read and write English to the tenth grade level.
2) Must have good communication skills.
3) Must want to be a trainer.
4) Must be patient, flexible, and understanding.
5) Must be able to explain things clearly.
6) Must be able to follow written lesson plans.

Job Description: OTJ Trainers

On top of regular job duties, OTJ trainers will

1) Deliver instruction to trainees as per written lesson plans.
2) Deliver immediate positive corrective feedback to trainees.
3) Administer evaluation instruments to trainees to assure training success.
4) Follow up training with coaching.

Training Topics

As experts, we have determined the following topics to be essential for a comprehensive train-the-trainer program. Our managers in the future may need to be able to design small training sessions for new procedures or changes that might require additional training for their staff. Managers will be conducting the training in their departments, so they must also be trained to use the lesson plans effectively. They will be training their own workers to be OTJ trainers. We will, therefore, design training to enable us to "conduct training utilizing the lesson plans." This training session will be administered to managers as a portion of their comprehensive trainer training, and they in turn can administer it to their department's OTJ trainers.

Upon completion of train-the-trainer training, the manager will be able to

1) Conduct needs assessments.
2) Construct job lists, objectives, and job breakdowns (task analysis).

3) Write lesson plans for training in their departments that incorporate the learning principles.

4) Conduct training utilizing the lesson plans.

Topic 4. Conduct Training: Upon completion of train-the-trainer training, Managers and OTJ trainers will be able to conduct training utilizing the lesson plans.

    4.a. Upon completion of the training, the trainee will be able to

        1. Identify training examples of the learning principles.

    4.b. Upon completion of the training, the trainee will be able to

        1. Conduct a demonstration of training using a lesson plan.

        2. Give immediate positive corrective feedback to the trainee.

Training Topic	Training Method	Trainer	Place Held
4. Conduct Training			
4.a.1. Learning Principles	Lecture/Discussion with handouts & exercises	Training Consultant (Mgrs. at later time)	Sm. Conf. Rm.
4.b.1. Demonstrate Lesson Plan	Demonstration With handout	Training Consultant (Mgrs. at later time)	Sm. Conf. Rm.
4.b.2. Immediate Corrective Feedback	Practice—Trainee Demos. with critiques	Training Consultant (Mgrs. at later time)	Sm. Conf. Rm.

Lesson Plans

We are ready to devise the lesson plans for Topic Four (Conducting Training). It is just one training segment of a much larger comprehensive training program for GTI managers. We are developing instruction for managers who will then use it to train the employees doing OTJ training in their departments. Because we are training employees who have the necessary characteristics to be successful trainers, the training can be completed in about two hours.

This textbook is education. It is designed to teach everything about training design. The instruction we are designing for Topic Four is not education. It is training and thus will be considerably less involved because OTJ trainers merely need to meet the objective, which is: "To be able to conduct training utilizing the lesson plans."

The lesson plan will begin with learning principles (4.a.1.). We have the list of learning principles from Chapter Seven, which will serve as content for our lesson. This list is the equivalent of task breakdown or task analysis.

Lesson Plan—Conduct Training

4.a.1. Learning Principles

4.b.1. Demonstration of Lesson Plan

4.b.2. Immediate Corrective Feedback

Time: To be scheduled when needed

Place: Small Conference Room

Trainer: Training Consultant (Managers at a later time)

Trainees: Managers (OTJ Trainers at a later time)

Method: Lecture/Discussion/Demonstration/Practice with handouts
       and exercises

Materials Needed:
- "Learning Principles" handouts, copied for each trainee
- Overhead transparency of "Learning Principles" handout
- Overhead Projector
- Copies of "Lesson Plan" to be handed out after the lecture
- Overhead transparency of "Learning Principles Lesson Plan" handout
- Marker to use on transparency
- Demonstration "Critique Form" handouts

Duration: About two hours

Objective: Upon completion of the training session, the trainee will be able to

1) List and give training examples of learning principles.

2) Deliver training using a lesson plan.

3) Give immediate corrective feedback.

Step	Procedure	Trainer's Directions
4.a.1.	Welcome and Agenda	"Hello everyone. Thanks for taking time from your busy schedules for this training session. Today we are going to go over how to conduct training using the lesson plans. [Learning Principle number six] We have spent a lot of time and money developing excellent training materials. We now must make sure that everyone who will be conducting training knows how to use them. [Learning Principle number five] The lesson plans will result in consistent training with everything covered that needs to be covered, and covered in the most effective ways."
4.b.1.	What we are going to study and why it is important	"We are going to spend the first twenty minutes looking at the Adult Principles of Learning. We adults are different from children. We have lots of experience and already know many things. We also have lots of baggage that can affect our openness to learning."
		To be good trainers, it is helpful for us to understand our trainees and the way they learn. That's the way for us to be most effective. [Hand out Learning Principles and, at the same time, say:] I am giving you copies of the Adult Learning Principles, and we are goiig to go through all of them."
	Learning Principles handout	"Most of this information will ring bells for you. It makes sense. We know how we learn and what we like. This is common sense stuff. It is a good idea, though, to review the principles and to see them all together on a list. It helps us to put our common knowledge into some type of framework that will help us to use it better."

(continues)

Step	Procedure	Trainer's Directions
	Learning Principles Overhead	[Put up Learning Principles transparency on the overhead projector and point to each of the principles as you explain each with the following instruction.]
1	Trainees prefer an informal atmosphere for training sessions where trainees are treated as professionals rather than as students.	[Read the Principle and then say:] "Some of our workers might not have had good school experiences. They may be afraid of failing or just dislike school in general. If our training feels like school, they might be afraid or not at all open to learning. Training is different from school, though." "In training, everyone has to get an A. Satisfactory is not okay. Can you imagine what would happen to our customers if only 70 percent of the time they got what they actually ordered for dinner, or got checked into their rooms properly, or went in and found that the room had been cleaned properly?" "It is our responsibility to make sure that every trainee masters the material. All of it, every time. We may have to go slower for some or think of a different way to explain it. But, they must all be on the same page before we let them loose on customers."
2	Trainees need encouragement and positive feedback as to their progress.	"Do not keep the trainees guessing. In a learning situation, we all want to know how we are progressing. As managers, we do not let them go in the wrong direction or do anything incorrectly. We immediately help them to get back on track. The idea is that they must learn the material, and it is our job to facilitate this."

Step	Procedure	Trainer's Directions
3	Trainees should not compete with each other.	"Not everyone is competitive. Some of our trainees might just give up instead of being inspired by competition. Also, we are trying to foster teamwork. That means we work together, not against each other. A trainee can certainly compete with him- or herself—like trying to beat his or her last time,
4	Trainees learn at different speeds and may need individual attention and training.	and so forth. Our trainees will learn at different speeds. That is okay so long as they learn it. Only highly competitive people are motivated by competition. Many trainees will not be highly competitive, though, so do not force them to compete."
5	Trainees must want to learn and understand why the material is necessary.	"We adults do not learn until we actually want to—until we see a good reason for it. I did not learn how to use e-mail until my best friend moved away and my phone bill was too high. As soon as I realized the advantage to me, I learned how to use it. Likewise, we need to let our trainees know *why* they need to learn and precisely *what* it is that we are trying to teach them. Basically, they need to see the point."
		"I started this training session by telling you why you needed to know the learning principles. Do you remember the reasons I gave you—why they are important— how they are useful to know? What were the reasons I gave?"
		[Let the trainees volunteer reasons. If none are forthcoming, try giving hints like, "Do we learn the same as children? How are we different?"]

(continues)

Step	Procedure	Trainer's Directions
6	Trainees must be told what they are to do and then be shown the sequential steps to do it.	"Our trainees are not mind readers. Most of us need to have an idea of where we are going so we can understand what we are doing. For example, if someone is giving us directions to get someplace in a car, we first like to know where we are going—the final destination. And then we like step-by-step directions, in order. Otherwise, it does not make sense. The idea is to help our trainees to *get* the material. So, we have to present it in such a way that they will."
7	The training should be related to trainees' life experiences.	"If we can relate training to something the trainee already knows, we can speed up the comprehension. Like the example I used a second ago of getting directions for driving someplace."
8	Trainees need real and tangible examples.	"We want to relate everything to what we already know. For one thing, it is more interesting. For another, it is familiar."
9	Trainees learn better by doing.	"Most of us learn better by actually doing the thing we are supposed to learn. Think about learning to tie your shoes or ride a bike. An explanation is probably useful, but a diagram or written instructions are not nearly as useful as actually *doing it.*"
10	Trainees should learn to do the activity correctly, then build up speed.	"We do not want to waste time doing things incorrectly. Get trainees going in the right direction and allow them to build up speed naturally. Most things our employees are doing and learning are physical actions. We do not want them practicing them wrong. They would eventually have to unlearn and then relearn the right way if we let them do it wrong at the beginning."

Step	Procedure	Trainer's Directions
11	Training should be conducted in numerous shorter sessions	"We know that children have short attention spans. But let us face it—so do we! Especially when we are learning things that we may not be especially excited about. So let us keep the sessions short so we do not lose them and just waste time."
12	Repetition and practice result in better retention.	If we call someone numerous times we usually end up knowing their phone number by heart. Repetition results in memorization. When we want someone to learn something, we should repeat it—a lot. We should have them repeat it or do it several times. The more they do, the better they will learn it."
13	Keep lag time short between time of training and the job.	"Most movies we have seen we can remember the next day. But with each day that passes, we remember less—it becomes less clear in our memories. Eventually, we may only vaguely remember that we saw it but not really any particulars about it. Personally, I have to re-read the portable phone manual every time I need to program a new phone number in the speed dial—because I do not do it often enough and forget how."
14	Use a combination of training methods.	"We learn better when we absorb things in a variety of ways. If we *hear, see, touch*, and *try* something . . . we are much more likely to remember it than if we simply *hear* it." "That is why we have these learning principles on a handout, on the overhead, and why I am talking about them. We will also do a little activity with them. It is repetition, people. Again, the point of training is that everyone must master the material, so we do whatever it takes."

(continues)

Step	Procedure	Trainer's Directions
15	Make the training interesting and relevant.	"This next bit is pretty obvious. If something is boring and pointless, we will not bother to remember it."
16	The trainer should be well prepared.	"We do not want the trainer to get in the way of the training. What I mean is that if our trainees are focused on the trainer instead of the material, for whatever reason, the training will be less effective. Training is part of the job, too. It is never acceptable to do any of our jobs below the standard. I am responsible for making sure you are well trained to train. You are responsible for your employees' performance."
17	The trainer must create a positive learning environment.	"We must provide an atmosphere that is conducive to learning. Our trainees must feel comfortable, not threatened or afraid, not stressed. They must feel *open* to learning, and it is our responsibility to be attuned to the atmosphere and adjust it if it is not conducive to learning."
18	The trainer must exhibit enthusiasm.	"As trainers, we are to a certain extent role models. What we do is far more important than what we say. Our enthusiasm should be catching. It is far more satisfying and easier to work when we feel some enthusiasm for it."
	Conclusion	"In retrospect, I do not think there was anything on that list you did not already know. It was just a lot of common sense. It is helpful, though, to consider all the principles together when we are going to try to train or teach adults. We can forget and fall back into old ways, even when they are not as effective. 'This is how I was trained,' we may think."

Step	Procedure	Trainer's Directions
	Activity	[Hand out a copy of the lesson plan for the Learning Principles, just delivered.]
	Learning Principles Lesson Plan Handout	"Take a couple of minutes to read over this. What I want you to do is identify every place in the lesson plan where a Learning Principle was used. Like where something was repeated or a real life example was used. Do it like this:"
	Overhead of Lesson Plan Example of first two learning principles in the lesson plan	[Put the first page of this lesson plan on the overhead and note the underlined portions in the trainer's directions followed by Learning Principle number six and number five in brackets.]
		"Well, what did you think of the lesson plan? Did it look familiar?" [Get reactions of trainees—they should note that it was almost identical to what was presented.] "Any one of you could take this lesson plan and present the exact same thing! That means that no matter how many times the training is delivered, or who delivers the training, it will be exactly the same. Every trainee will get exactly the same material in the same way. That is the beauty of a lesson plan."
		"To be honest, it did take a long time to put this thing together—but, it takes *no* time to do it the second time. It is already put together. I just review it and get all the handouts and transparencies and the marker, and I am ready to go."
		[Using the overhead of the lesson plan and the marker] "Let us go through this lesson plan from the beginning and underline all the examples you underlined of the Learning Principles used."

(continues)

Step	Procedure	Trainer's Directions
	Discussion	[Ask trainees] "Do you think the use of the Learning Principles made the lesson better? How? Could we incorporate other Learning Principles in this instruction? Which ones and how?"
4.b.2	Practice—Immediate Corrective Feedback Demonstration Critique Form	"We are going to break here and meet again [give time and date]. In the meantime, you have an *assignment*! You are going to choose a short ten-minute training segment from the training documents for your department and prepare to present it at our next session. You will train us just like you would train a new employee or as one of your OTJ trainers would train a new employee. We will critique the training delivery and the training lesson plan, and we will look for the use of Learning Principles. The idea is to get a chance to practice using a lesson plan, and become more familiar with the process. [Hand out Demonstration Critique Form] We will use the Demonstration Critique Form to help us analyze each other's performance in the demonstration next time. A critique form helps us to focus on some of the things that we need to do in a demonstration. It also helps us to critique in an objective way. Critiques should be helpful and certainly not harmful in any way. . . . So, I would like you to go ahead and critique my performance on the lesson I just delivered. Do not put your names on them because I am going to collect them, and we will go over them before we leave." [Collect them and discuss the results.]
	Closing	"Any questions? Comments? Do you understand what you need to have ready for next time? Thank you and we will meet again on [say time and date]."

Handout: The Principles of Adult Learning

Principles	Examples/Notes
1) Trainees prefer an informal atmosphere for training sessions where trainees are treated as professionals rather than students.	
2) Trainees need encouragement and positive feedback as to their progress.	
3) Trainees should not compete with each other.	
4) Trainees learn at different speeds and may need individual attention and training.	
5) Trainees must want to learn and understand why the material is necessary.	
6) Trainees must be told what they are to do and then be shown the sequential steps to do it.	
7) The training should be related to trainees' life experiences.	
8) Trainees need real and tangible examples.	
9) Trainees learn better by doing.	
10) Trainees should learn to do the activity correctly, then build up speed.	
11) Training should be conducted in numerous shorter sessions.	
12) Repetition and practice result in better retention.	

(continues)

13) Keep lag time short between time of training and the job.

14) Use a combination of training methods.

15) Make the training interesting and relevant.

16) The trainer should be well prepared.

17) The trainer must create a positive learning environment.

18) The trainer must exhibit enthusiasm.

Demonstration Critique Form

	No		Yes
	1	2	3

Name of the Lesson:_____

Were you told:

• What you were going to learn?	1	2	3
• Why it is important?	1	2	3
• Why you need to know this?	1	2	3
• When you will use this?	1	2	3
• Was it presented in a logical sequence?	1	2	3
• Was the trainer prepared?	1	2	3
• Did the trainer check for trainee comprehension?	1	2	3
• How?_____			
• Could everyone see and hear?	1	2	3
• Was the pace just right? Not too fast or slow?	1	2	3
• Did you learn what you were expected to learn?	1	2	3
• Did the trainer have any distracting mannerisms?	1	2	3

- What were they?_____
- Does this performance need improvement?   1   2   3
- How could this performance be improved?_____

_____

Comments:_____

CONCLUSION

The Topic Four lesson plan took about six hours to construct. Training design is expensive. That is one of the reasons why needs assessment is so important. If we spend the time and money, we want to make sure we are designing the right training. Once the training is designed, however, it results in consistent, convenient, efficient, and effective training.

It is essential that we take the extra time to train everyone who will be using documents (the lesson plans) to deliver training. Training is a learned skill, and, without instruction on how to do it, the trainer may not be able to utilize documents effectively. Training the trainer also takes time and money. Training is expensive so we must assure (through proper training) that the money spent is not wasted.

Some of our employees assume training responsibilities as part of their jobs. We understand the necessity of training employees to make beds, check-in guests, and take drink orders. We also have to train our employees to train if they have training responsibilities added to their jobs. As professionals, we reduce as much chance and risk as possible. For training to be effective, the trainers must know how to train. They learn that from train-the-trainer training.

CHAPTER THOUGHT QUESTIONS

1. Explain why it is necessary to teach employees (with training responsibilities) how to train. What are possible problems if trainers have not been trained to train?

2. Think about instructors you have had in school who did not seem to be very good teachers. What did they do or not do that made them less effective? What could they have done differently to be better? Do you think they were taught how to teach?

3. Think about training you have received at the various jobs you've held. Choose the worst and the best and compare and contrast. Who trained you? How did this person train you? Do you think the trainer was an effective trainer? Why or why not? What could have improved the trainer's performance? Do you think the trainer had been trained to train?

4. List the characteristics necessary to be an effective trainer and discuss each individually, explaining why the characteristic is necessary.

5. Review and list the Adult Learning Principles in Chapter Seven. Discuss why it is necessary for trainers to understand and incorporate the principles in their training activities.

6. Describe the process for designing training for trainers using the Training Design Model. Please outline all the steps and relate the process to designing training for any line position.

7. Review Chapters Three and Four. Please define needs assessment and then list and describe all the steps in needs assessment—what information is necessary and how and where do we get it.

8. Chapter Eleven was about designing training for a new trainer. The process, however, follows the same model as designing training for any line position. Apply all the steps in question number seven and come up with a needs assessment plan for designing training for a housekeeper in a hotel, or institution. What are the questions you will need to ask and whom will you ask?

9. Pretend that you actually collected all the data called for in your needs assessment plan in question number eight. Using made-up data, devise a training plan for the housekeeper position according to the directions in Chapter Eight.

10. We can develop some very good-looking training by utilizing our own experience and knowledge. It takes a lot less time if we skip the data collection. Why, if we really do know how to do the job, do we still need to do a needs assessment as the first step in the training design?

12 Implementing Training and Evaluation

OBJECTIVES

We design training only if we will be able to utilize it again and again. It is too expensive and labor intensive to bother with if only one or two people will be trained. Large companies, however, that have steady turnover will use the training documents repeatedly. Each time the training documents are used, the trainee will receive the same high quality training, and the initial cost of training design is spread thinner.

We did a needs assessment to determine whether training would correct particular problems and to determine what type of training might be appropriate for particular situations. Once training is designed, we must determine that it corrected problems and did so in the most effective and efficient manner. We evaluate the program to ensure it is working, and then make any adjustments, modifications, or corrections necessary for its optimum effectiveness.

Every person we hire must be trained. Every person we train must successfully complete the training—that is, be able to perform a job according to certain standards before being expected to take the floor. We must design measures to determine whether each trainee has met the training objectives, and we must determine if the training was appropriate and satisfactory.

Upon completion of Chapter 12, the student should be able to

- Discuss the importance and necessity of all trainees mastering the training.

- Devise appropriate measures to determine whether the objectives have been attained.
- Discuss the importance and necessity of evaluating the training program.
- Describe the methods of evaluation for training programs.

Utilizing Training Documents

When we hire a new employee, we pull out the training documents—the training plan and lesson plans. Copies of the lesson plans are given to employees who will be conducting training. The training plan is shared with all involved (including the trainee) so that everyone knows exactly what is going on, when it occurs, and where it is to take place. Each trainer will have been trained to train and should now be ready to instruct new employees.

The trainer reviews the lesson plan, securing any necessary materials, handouts, and equipment. The lesson is practiced in advance so that the trainer is familiar and comfortable with the material. The more the trainer practices, the smoother the presentation. If most job duties stay the same, the training will not change much over time, and we will become very adept at performing it. As we go through the training the first time, we can note any modifications that need to be made so it goes better the next.

Constructing lesson plans is time-consuming. It only needs to be done once, though, and exists thereafter for each time we need to train a new employee. We only have to review the documents before we begin training. The lesson plan tells us everything we need for the lesson so we can be well prepared. The training is the same each time we administer it. We may feel funny about saying the same things over and over, but each trainee will have heard it only once, and all recipients of the identical training are getting exactly what they need in order to adequately perform their job duties. Once the lesson plans are written, they are extremely convenient to use and result in superior training—every time.

Mastering the Training

Of utmost importance is that trainees master the training. No matter how smooth our presentation is, we must stay attuned to our trainees to ensure they are understanding the material—and that they will be proficient at whatever it is we are teaching them to do. Learning principles were incorporated into the training materials in the design phase and, if utilized, should result in mastery. It is the trainer's responsibility, however, to assure this mastery. We can check for trainee comprehension throughout the instruction by asking trainees to repeat what we have said or explain the process in their own words, and, of course, by having them perform their job while we give immediate positive corrective feedback.

Immediate positive corrective feedback involves observation of trainees as they perform a new task. Trainers will be required to stand by and provide coaching to ensure that their charges perform duties in the proper manner. We must never allow trainees to do something incorrectly as it encourages similar behavior in the future and is in general a waste of time. If we notice a trainee practicing a task incorrectly, we immediately guide them back on the right path. There is no "discovery learning" in training. We tell them what we want them to do, we show them how we want it done, we let them attempt the duty themselves, and we make sure it is done the proper way.

Our trainees are not mind readers. They may not know how to do a new job duty the prescribed way before we show them how. If we allow them to do it incorrectly and then humiliate them in any way for not doing it the right way or fast enough, we are not fostering trust or teamwork, or using the most effective means of training. Everyone we hire and train must learn how to do their jobs in training. If a trainee is incapable of successfully completing the training, we are still responsible for that employee because we made a hiring mistake. We cannot let an employee do a job if he or she cannot meet the standards. To do so would be a costly mistake.

If we ask our employees, "Do you understand how to do this?" They may say, "Oh, yes," but still not really comprehend. We must ensure that they can do what we want them to do before they leave the training. We also must ensure that they can meet the objectives. Stating these training objectives is one of the first steps in training design. We state what the trainee will be able to do upon completion of the training. These objectives help us to stay on task and only teach the necessities. Objectives also help us to determine how something should be taught and how we should measure the outcomes of the training program.

One of the objectives for the cook's training at The Garden Terrace Inn (GTI) was: Upon completion of the training session, the trainee will be able to break eggs as per GTI standards. The lesson plan (in Chapter Nine) for breaking eggs begins with the previous objective and ends with "Evaluation:

On Day Three of training, have trainees go through all eight steps by themselves. Give immediate corrective feedback if necessary to ensure that it is done correctly."

The lesson plan in Chapter Eleven for conducting training begins with the following objective: "Upon completion of training session, trainee will be able to

- List and give training examples of the learning principles.
- Deliver training using a lesson plan.
- Give immediate corrective feedback."

The training was designed to meet the objectives. A lecture with activities was utilized to address the learning principles. Trainees were given copies of the lesson plan and asked to review it and note where the learning principles were utilized. The test was the activity at the end of the lesson plan. It required trainees to choose a lesson plan from their own department training documents and then present it to the rest of the managers being trained to train.

Much of the training for hospitality line jobs involves procedures. We *explain* the procedure, *show* them the procedure, *watch* them do the procedure, and give immediate positive corrective *feedback* to ensure that they are able to correctly do the procedure themselves. The objective is to be able to *do* the procedure upon completion of the training. The test to see if the objective has been met is to have them do the procedure themselves. If they can, they go to the job. If they cannot, we provide them with more training until they can perform their duties correctly.

The Four Levels of Evaluation

We evaluate four separate things in training. The first level of evaluation is whether or not the trainee mastered the session's material. This evaluation is part of the lesson plan and is a type of test. This test often looks like instruction. The instruction is designed to enable trainees to meet an objective. We may use demonstration and practice to teach our employees how to do something. The test might be having employees perform a job themselves. The trainer gives the trainee a test at the end of the session.

The second level of evaluation has to do with whether the training was to the employees' liking. Was it presented in the best possible way? Did the trainees learn the material in spite of the trainer or did the trainer facilitate the learning process? We evaluate the delivery method and materials by asking, "Could the trainer have been better or more well-received by the trainees?" The trainees are questioned after the training (either verbally or in writing) to get their input on the presentation. We may find that the trainer spoke too fast, mumbled, or was not well prepared. We also could discover that the pace was too fast or slow, that there was no chance to ask questions, or that questions were ignored or treated with disdain. We, of course, also could find out that the training was fun and a great experience for the trainees.

The trainees could have experienced terrific training, learned everything, but got out on the job and found they had been trained in unnecessary things. Or, perhaps they were not trained in things they really needed to know. The third level of evaluation finds out if the presentation's subject matter was the right subject matter. The trainer, designer, or the manager could ask the trainees' supervisor whether the newly trained employees came out of the training with all the skills necessary to do the job. Trainees also could be questioned after working their jobs for a while to find out if they have received any unnecessary training or if there were things they did need but did not get in the training.

The fourth and last thing we need to evaluate is whether the training actually corrected the problem for which it was designed. In needs assessment, we might have determined that our high turnover rates were related to inadequate training. Once we have designed and implemented the new training, we must compare the pre- and post-training turnover rates. Did they go down? If they did (and nothing else changed), we can assume that the training made a positive difference. If the turnover rates did not go down, we need to figure out why. Was anything else going on that could have resulted in higher turnover rates? If we cannot find any reason for the rates to not have gone down, we are forced to admit that the training did not fix the problem. We may have wasted a lot of time and money designing unnecessary training. This is why a needs assessment is so essential. Before we design any training program, we need to make sure that it is what we really need. Afterward we must check to ensure that it really did work. Training is costly to design and implement, so we will have to justify the expense.

The whole point of the evaluation is to see what our employees have learned from the training . . . and to make any adjustments, modifications, or improvements necessary to meet the original desire, objective, or need. Again, professionals take out the guesswork and any unnecessary risk for management. Evaluations enable us to know exactly what happened in training and to make any corrections that will make it better next time. If we do not conduct an evaluation, we will be merely guessing at how things are and what we might like to change. Or, we might not even know that we need to make a change. That is scary when we are trying to compete with professionals who have done a needs assessment and evaluation and know exactly where they are and what they need to do.

Test Criteria

We use all different methods of tests to evaluate. All tests must have certain characteristics, no matter what type of test we use. The test has to be **valid**, that is, the test should measure what it is supposed to measure. A valid test in training will show that the trainee met the objective. A test also must be **reliable**, or consistent. A reliable test will always measure the same thing the same way. A valid test will always be reliable, but a reliable test will not always be valid. We can have a very reliable test—say, a test that indicates how much algebra everyone who takes the test knows. If we are using the test to see if someone is an adequate server, the test would not be valid because a server does not usually need to know much algebra to be successful in the position. The test is consistent. We get very reliable data on algebra knowledge. However, the test is not appropriate if we are trying to evaluate servers.

Tests also should be **objective**. Objective tests are not left up to guesswork or interpretation. They are observable. Using these tests, we can compare something to a tangible standard. We do not ask, "How do we feel about this employee's performance?" Instead, we match an employee's performance to the standard. After training, the employee is supposed to crack eggs using the eight steps. The trainee either can or cannot. It has nothing to do with how hard the trainee is trying, how much we like the trainee, or how well everyone else is able to do the task.

Tests also must be **practical**. If the tests are too confusing, complex, or try to measure too many things at once, they will not be very useful. We may not even bother using them. Or, we may use them, but those taking the tests may not understand them, and their answers will be unreliable. Those analyzing the test results might not be able to make sense of them. We want to keep tests simple, to the point of the objective, clear, and easy to administer and grade.

Evaluation Instruments or Activities

We evaluate

1. Level of learning from the training
2. Acceptability and quality of the training delivery
3. The validity of training (Was it the right information needed to do the job?)
4. Whether the training corrected the problem for which it was designed

We construct or design evaluation instruments or activities to assess these four levels of evaluation. The instruments or activities must be valid, reliable, objective, and practical. We will now look at possible evaluation instruments or activities that might be appropriate for the four levels of evaluation.

Level One Evaluation Instruments or Activities

Level one evaluation asks: Did the trainee meet the objective of the training? The evaluation instrument or activity is part of the lesson plan and can be in the form of a test. The test can be written, verbal, or a physical activity, but it must be appropriate for the trainee and the job.

Training for most line positions involves teaching employees to do some physical activity (such as making a bed, checking in a guest, or taking a drink order). The test should match the objective. If the objective states that the trainee should be able to make a bed as per hotel specifications, the test should be to make a bed as per the hotel's specification. We want them to make the bed, not understand how to make a bed or to be able to explain how to make a bed, but to *make* the bed. If we give them a written or oral test describing how to make the bed, that does not actually test that they can make the bed. Rather, it would test whether or not they could *describe* making the bed.

We could actually write the objective and devise the final test (for the objective) before designing the instruction. We sometimes hear people talking about "teaching to the test" as something less than desirable. If we want students or trainees to know something specific and that something specific is what they will be tested on, does it not make sense to teach it to

172 Training Design for the Hospitality Industry

them? What else would we teach them? Of course, we are going to teach to the test.

If we want dishwashers to be able to properly fill dishwasher racks, the test would be to fill a dishwasher rack properly. We could give them a written test or have them draw dishes on a diagram of a dish rack, but neither is as sensible or as valid as having them actually fill the dish rack with real dishes. Also, reading and writing may not be requirements for many line jobs. If we expect an employee to take a test, they may not be able to. Therefore, their failure would not be an indication of job competency, but rather that they could not read and write adequately. The test would be invalid because it would be testing literacy instead of job skills.

If our objective was that the trainee should be able to check a guest in (again, that is a physical procedure), then a physical activity would be a more appropriate test than a written or verbal test. We, however, do not want to have our trainees being tested on customers. A proper test might be to simulate a check-in opportunity. The trainer or manager could pretend to check in, and trainees could perform the operation in an almost real situation.

A simulation would be an appropriate way to test whether servers have met their training objectives. Mock serving situations could be staged to enable trainees to be tested without exposing guests to possible mishaps or confusion. We want our tests to be as close to the real thing as possible. The idea of the test is to ensure that the trainee has mastered the object of the training. The further the test is from the reality of the job, the less assurance we have that the employee can actually do the task.

A verbal or written test might be appropriate for cooks in sanitation training. Time and temperature ratios, cross contamination, HACCP standards, and so forth can be tested on paper. It is necessary, however, for us to realize that learning from lectures and books oftentimes is not transferred to the reality of the job. We can test that trainees have the knowledge, but then we also must watch for, supervise, and coach our employees to use the information as it was meant for the job. The written or verbal test is part of the training documents and is included in the lesson plan.

A combination of tests might be useful for certain objectives. We might give housekeepers a written test on cleaning agents so we are assured that they can recognize them, which then can be followed by a physical test for actually using the cleaning agents. If our housekeeping staff does not read and write English as a first language, the written test could involve pictures of the cleaning agent to be matched with the corresponding bathroom fixture for which it was designed. The physical test would be for the housekeepers to actually clean a vacated room to the hotel's specification. The written, picture-matching test is one of the training documents and the physical test is described in the lesson plan.

There are no rules here. We have to use our heads to determine the best way to evaluate whether trainees have met specific objectives. Most of this is quite simple. If we want them to be able to do something, we design training that tells, shows, and then lets them practice it. We test for competency by having them do the thing themselves. If they do it right, they can go on the job; if not, more training is needed.

Level Two Evaluation Instruments or Activities

The acceptability and quality of training delivery can be found in two ways. A manager or training expert might observe the training to critique trainers and determine if they could improve upon the delivery. It would be useful to have a form such as the Demonstration Critique Form (from Chapter Eleven) to reduce any subjectivity and to ensure that trainers are evaluated consistently and on relevant criteria. We must keep in mind that the purpose of the evaluation is to improve the training. It is never to catch someone doing something wrong or to punish or humiliate them. Evaluation is positive and should not be perceived as threatening.

Once the trainees have experienced the training, their input should be requested. We must assure our trainees that their opinions are needed to improve training and that their opinions will in no way be used against them. A written questionnaire is convenient for collecting this type of information if the trainees have the reading and writing skills necessary to complete them. Questionnaires might be appropriate for front desk personnel, servers, and cooks because those positions require reading and writing skills.

We also are interested in the opinions of employees who have gone through training but whose English skills are less developed. We might choose to interview employees and verbally ask questions from the questionnaire (in the appropriate language). We will either devise a questionnaire or a list of questions to be asked in an interview. The questionnaire is part of the training program and is reused each time that training is delivered. Asking employees about the quality of the training helps us to keep the quality high and also lets employees know we care about their opinions and their experiences in our operations.

We could modify the Demonstration Critique Form from Chapter Eleven to use for the trainee questionnaire. These or similar questions need to be asked so that we can improve the trainers' delivery, if necessary.

Training Critique Form

	No		Yes
	<u>1</u>	2	<u>3</u>

Name of the Trainer:_____

Training Topic:_____

- Were you told what you were going to learn?   1   2   3
- Were you told why it is important?   1   2   3
- Were you told why you need to know this?   1   2   3
- Were you told when you will use this?   1   2   3
- Was it presented in a logical sequence?   1   2   3
- Was the trainer prepared?   1   2   3
- Did the trainer check if you were understanding?   1   2   3
  How?_____
- Could you see and hear?   1   2   3
- Was the pace just right? Not too fast or slow?   1   2   3
- Did you learn what you were expected to learn?   1   2   3
- Did the trainer have any distracting mannerisms?   1   2   3
  What were they?_____
- Does this training need improvement?   1   2   3
- How could this training be improved?_____
  _____
- Comments:_____

Level Three Evaluation Instruments or Activities

Once trainees have successfully completed the training and gone on to their jobs, we can ask them if they were given the right training needed to do the job. We also can ask their supervisors if the training properly prepared the trainees to do their jobs. If the jobs do not change, we may only have to ask these questions periodically (or when something changes). If we did a thorough needs assessment and collected all the job data (job lists and task analysis), we probably have the right information in the training. It is best to check this information, however, because at this point it may only require some simple modifications to correct deficiencies or excesses.

Level Four Evaluation Instruments or Activities

We must ascertain whether the training corrected the problem for which it was designed. If we had no previous training, the existence of the newly designed training program is adequate to determine that we solved the no-training problem. If, however, we designed training to decrease the rates of turnover, customer complaints, accidents, and so forth, then we must compare the pre- and post-training statistics to determine any difference. Obviously, we need pre-training statistics to do this. We should have collected them in the needs assessment phase. We cannot say we have high turnover or accident rates that training will reduce if we do not have statistics showing these figures. The statistics are used to warrant designing training.

A level four evaluation is only done once. We want to keep an eye on turnover, or the accident rate, or whatever problem our training corrected, but if the levels were to rise again, it would be necessary to do another needs assessment to determine the cause. We cannot assume that the reason would stay the same.

Cost of Training

When we perform a level four evaluation, we also have to consider the cost of training design. The solution may cost more than the problem. We may not be able to justify the training, if this is the case. We have to be able to put a dollar amount on the problem. What does a high rate of turnover cost us? We have to think in terms of rehiring, retraining, reduced service levels, customer dissatisfaction, employee dissatisfaction, manager burnout, and so on. We have to determine the cost of the training. We can get an estimate from a training design consultant, or, if we design the training ourselves, we can add up all the hours spent in collecting data and design. Those are the hours in which we were not doing our other job duties. Chapter Fourteen will address these costs in more detail.

We also have to consider the cost of implementing training. Someone is being trained to train. That training takes the person off his or her own job and someone else is conducting the training. Trainers are spending their time training instead of performing their other job duties. We have to add in the cost of all supplies, training materials, and copies. The trainee is being paid to train and is not producing until they are finished with the program.

We must keep track of all these costs in order to compare the total cost of training with the cost of not training. Initially, the cost of training may be more than the cost of the problem. Over time, though, the cost of training is spread thinner and is mostly a one-time expense. The savings from training implementation can go on and on.

CONCLUSION

Training takes time and money to develop and implement. Professionals evaluate every aspect of the training to ensure that they are getting their money's worth. We cannot modify or fix training if we do not know what is wrong with it. We will not know there is anything wrong with it if we do not evaluate it.

Evaluation is very much like needs assessment except that it is done after the fact instead of before. A needs assessment looks at what we have *before* and what we need, and then we do something to fill in the discrepancy. Evaluation looks at what we have *after* and how it compares with what we wanted, and then does something to correct the discrepancy. We cannot evaluate anything without comparing it to something else. In business, we are generally comparing things to standards.

While we are using some fairly rigorous research methods to make our evaluations, the methods make sense if we keep in mind what we are trying to find out. Evaluation is one of our most important control tools and is the process most often neglected.

KEY WORDS

Immediate positive corrective feedback

Valid

Reliable

Objective

Practical

CHAPTER THOUGHT QUESTIONS

1. Describe the training documents and how you use them when you hire a new employee. Detail the benefits of having training documents.

2. Discuss the difference between education and training in terms of mastering the material. Describe the techniques for checking trainee comprehension throughout a training program.

3. Discuss the relationship between the behavioral objective and the test at the end of the training topic instruction. Give examples of the types of behavioral objectives in hospitality line positions and their appropriate tests. What happens if a trainee cannot meet the objective at the end of the training?

4. Define evaluation. Discuss the purpose of evaluation and why it is important. What is the difference between an evaluation and a needs assessment? How are they similar?

5. List and define the four levels of evaluation. Discuss why each level needs to be evaluated.

6. All evaluation tests must be valid, reliable, objective, and practical. Define and discuss each of the four test criteria for the evaluation tests. Use examples from your own classes and/or work experience.

7. List and describe the level one evaluation instruments or activities. Use examples from your own education and/or work experience.

8. List and describe the level two evaluation instruments or activities. Use examples from your own education and/or work experience.

9. List and describe the level three evaluation instruments or activities. Use examples from your own education and/or work experience.

10. List and describe the level four evaluation instruments or activities. Use examples from your own education and/or work experience.

13   *Coaching and Counseling*

OBJECTIVES

The supervision of employees means ongoing training. We get our trainees functioning at standards before they leave the training, and then we ensure they stay functioning at that same level once they return to their jobs. We do this through coaching and counseling.

Upon completion of Chapter 13, the student should be able to

- Discuss the importance of coaching and counseling.
- Define and describe coaching and counseling techniques.

Motivation

We hear managers and teachers talk about motivating their employees or students. However, we do not really motivate anyone to do anything. We are, instead, motivated by our own individual needs. **Motivation** is the galvanizing force behind why we do things. We all have similar emotions and feelings that vary in intensity. As a result, our individual needs are not infinite and may be categorized, depending on where we are in our lives.

The idea is to figure out what motivates people and then provide it, contingent upon them doing what we want them to do. When we were young and poor, we may have thought that money was the most important factor in job satisfaction. If one does not have adequate money, it is the most important factor. But, as soon as we had enough money, other things became important, such as autonomy, supervision styles, recognition, job duties, career opportunities, benefits, vacation time, flexibility, and so forth. At first, we may have been willing to do just about anything if we were paid enough. However, that level of satisfaction does not last and other things become more important.

Because people are more alike than different, we are all capable of relating to each other. We can understand what others are feeling. We can understand if someone has been unemployed, has no family, has a broken car or no car, has no assets, or has a small child to care for, that he or she might feel overwhelmed with fear and/or anxiety. As managers, our purpose is to get our staff to do what we want them to do and to do it graciously. In order to do this, we must recognize where our employees are and figure out what motivates them. We must let go of blame or judgmental thinking because that will only be an obstacle to our getting what we want.

The employee in the previous example, due to his or her current life situation, is most likely in need of money or some sort of financial stability. For a job well done, we can provide the money and stability. We have to match the reward to what the employee considers to be a reward. A young manager might be excited at the prospect of dinner at the GM's home—they may view it as a chance to become better acquainted and to enhance their chances for promotion. The employee in the previous paragraph, however, might find the thought of dinner at the GM's home terrorizing. It could cause hardship in terms of assembling the appropriate clothes and paying for transportation and child care. Rather than being viewed as a reward, it might be seen as undesirable. It could even cause the employee to quit the job.

If we pay attention to our employees and really listen to what they say about themselves, we will be able to ascertain where they are in their lives, what their concerns are, and what they need from their jobs. Once we are past the bottom-line survival issues (such as food and shelter), other things become important. If we are starving, we do not really care what we eat or where it comes from. Once we are no longer starving, though, it is unlikely that any of us would choose to eat from a garbage can. If it is winter and we have no shoes, we are unlikely to turn down a free pair of ugly brown oxfords. We get a little more particular about what we wear, however, when we are beyond the dire poverty stage.

Popularity is of little concern to homeless people. Once we are financially stable, however, we would probably be interested in having friends and a social life. Employees who are at this level will perhaps enjoy social events such as company parties or softball teams. We can provide these types of social opportunities to motivate our employees who need social opportunities.

Employees who are financially stable and have lots of friends may respond positively to special recognition such as an "employee of the month" plaque. The employee who is struggling to survive would rather have the money that the plaque cost, and the lonely employee also would not take much comfort in engraved accolades. Our stable employee with friends, however, could feel appreciated, energized, proud, and very motivated by receiving this recognition.

We must know our employees to figure out what motivates them. More autonomy or responsibility might give some employees a real thrill, while others may resent it. We cannot assume that our employees will respond to the same things that motivate us. They may not be in the same place in life as we are. They may have different needs—needs that we can certainly recognize and understand if we make the effort to get to know them.

Knowing our employees does not mean being best friends with them. It means listening to, watching, and becoming attuned to them, which we are all capable of doing. We may have to practice, though, to become adept at noticing. The benefit to us if we do this is that we will know what motivates our employees and be able to offer it as a reward for their good work. Our employees will feel cared about and appreciated, and they will do better work and stay longer on the job. We all like to be recognized for who we really are rather than just being seen as one of a crowd. We can bring out the best in our employees. Managers in the hospitality industry manage people. To successfully manage people, we must know and understand our people.

Diversity

Jealousy, grief, elation, fear, shame, and so on, are human emotions that cross all cultural boundaries. We, as managers, also experience the same emotions. How we respond to the emotions or how they are triggered can vary along cultural and gender lines. Different cultures have different communication styles and rules. Etiquette rules are not universal. What is polite in one culture might be found offensive in another. Most of us are primarily familiar with our own culture and may be uncomfortable with less familiar ones.

Diversity (differences between people, particularly in age, race, religion, and/or national origin) in the workplace is a fact of life. We are told to "celebrate diversity." We, of course, do not have to celebrate diversity.

But, if we do not, then we have made a choice to be less successful managers. If we do not have diversity in our employees, we may have to look at our hiring practices and ask ourselves if we are in any way restricting our selections by discriminating against specific members of society. The makeup of the labor pool has changed over the years and is quite diverse. We compete for employees and cannot afford to disregard whole groups of people, not to mention the fact that it is immoral and illegal to do so.

Our main task as managers is to get our employees to do what we want them to do, and this requirement may be foreign to them. It is necessary for us to effectively communicate with our employees to ensure they know what we want them to do. Even within our own familiar culture, we may have communication difficulties if we fail to recognize the differences in our employees. One employee may prefer a straightforward command, while another may require a softer "kid-glove" approach in order to get the same response.

If we choose to treat everyone the same, not everyone will respond in the same way. The idea is to get the same very positive, enthusiastic response from everyone, which means we will have to approach each person individually. While our underlying feelings are the same, the outward manifestations of our feelings can be quite different. We must be attuned to how individual employees will respond. We will make mistakes because we are human, but we will make fewer mistakes if we take the time to consider employees as individuals. We must recognize their styles so we can approach them in styles to which they will respond positively.

It is useful to understand the obvious cultural characteristics of our employees. All members of one particular culture, though, are not the same, and we must be attuned to the more subtle differences between individuals. A single-style approach to management and communication was never terribly effective, but it was feasible because our employees and customers did not have many options. Today, however, employees and customers can go elsewhere if they are not satisfied with our establishments, and they will.

Communication

The ability to speak, hear, and/or write does not necessarily result in effective communication. **Communication**, or conveying and receiving messages, is by definition a two-way street—meaning that for successful communication, the information must be received as it was intended to be received. We have no control over how or if it will be received. The only control we have is over what and how we communicate something. Therefore, it behooves us to learn to communicate in the most effective way possible.

Our employees also should be encouraged to communicate with us. This means that we need to be able to listen and hear what they are trying to tell us. They may not be practicing effective communication themselves, so we may have to find the hidden meanings in their messages. We want to ensure we are hearing the message and not responding to the messenger. We do not want to risk missing vital information because we assumed that the dish person or housekeeper was not very smart or would have nothing useful to offer.

Employees must feel safe in sharing information or ideas with management. Otherwise, they will not offer them. As managers, we have to practice listening and paying attention to what others are telling us. We cannot be thinking about our response to them (or, worse yet, what we are going to have for dinner that night) while they are trying to tell us something. We must listen and pay attention, which takes discipline to do. It also is one of the greatest gifts we can give to people—to actually listen to them. Not everything employees tell us will be of value. If we do not listen, though, we will miss all of it.

In business and personal relationships, there are times when we are trying to make a point or to get someone to change or do something. Rather than just open our mouths and assume we are communicating, it is a good idea to think first about what and how we are going to do this. We may want to assess our level of communication skills and perhaps make some changes. The following steps will result in more effective communication.

Determine What We Really Want

The first step is to identify precisely what we want to communicate. We ask ourselves what we are feeling, what we need to happen, and what we want. In business, *what we want* is often quite clear. "I want you to be on time for your shift." In personal relationships, our wants might not be so clear. This first step may be the most difficult because we have to dig through layers of expectations, disappointments, and unrecognized baggage to get at the truth.

If this is a new process and the outcomes are important, we may want to go through the steps in writing. We would most likely prepare and rehearse for an important speech. We also should consider preparing and rehearsing for important encounters or confrontations. The main point of good communication skills is to get someone to do what we want.

We must ask ourselves if what we want is feasible and ethical. If the other person is completely incapable of doing what we want, we are wasting our time pursuing this end. As managers and civilized people, we have the responsibility to determine whether or not what we want is appropriate, beneficial to all involved, and legal. If it is not, we must not pursue our want. With management comes the responsibility of self-regulation.

How Do We Get What We Want?

The second step is to use our brains and figure out the best way to get what we want. If we want someone to do something and we do not communicate this desire to the other person, it might not happen. We cannot assume that people are mind readers. We are often asking people to do things they do not want to do, so it is unreasonable to expect them to decide on their own to go ahead and do it.

Effective communication is straightforward and put into terms that the receiver can accept. Using guilt or threats is not straightforward and not nearly as effective. We have to state what we want in a way that enables the receiver to hear the message that we are trying to convey. If we want someone to be more gracious with our prospective guests on the phone, we need to give them a specific request with specific examples so they know what it is we expect. If we say something like, "You are not very nice and need to do better," the employee would most likely focus on the *you are not very nice* part. They might be hurt or angry, and as a result, probably would not try to do better. The employee maybe is not very nice, but if we attack them, they will most likely respond to the attack instead of the request for change.

To get what we want, we must let go of anger and blame so that the other person can hear our message. People tend to react to blame and anger with countering blame and anger, which, of course, does not get us what we want. We should instead say something like, "You represent the hotel to our prospective guests who call for information. Please remember to call them by their names so that the phone conversation feels more personal." This approach has a much better chance of working because we have not attacked or insulted the employee. We have told the employee precisely what it is that we want them to do, and why it is important.

Anytime we want people to change something, we must consider if they have the ability to do so. We may need to train them so that they can learn how to do the new activity, and then give them the opportunity to practice this new behavior before trying it on customers.

Supervision

Managers are responsible for ensuring that all jobs are performed correctly and that the customers are satisfied. The original standards for the operation were determined by management to match the expectations and desires of customers. The standards of employees, however, may not be the same as the customers. We train our employees to perform to the customer standards and then use **supervision** to ensure that these standards do not erode over time. If our customers are not satisfied—if their expectations and desires are not met—they will go elsewhere and our business will suffer.

Coaching and counseling are supervisory tools that we use to keep our employees on track. Both require an applied knowledge of motivational theory and communication skills.

Coaching

Coaching is ongoing reinforcement of standards with positive feedback. Athletic or drama coaches watch the action closely and give the athlete or actor encouragement, praise, and/or tips for improvement before and after their performance. We do the same in supervision. We watch what our employees are doing. We praise them when they do their jobs well, and we correct them when they are veering away from standards.

As managers, we use **reinforcement** to reward employees for good behavior. Most people do not like meaningless compliments, but they do like, and perhaps, need appreciation and recognition when it is deserved. If we never tell employees that we like things that they are doing, they may not continue doing them. "Why bother?" might be the attitude, or they might not know that they were doing good things. We should not assume that our employees know what we think. We must tell them. We must tell them when they are doing things well so that they will continue to do them. We must tell them when they are not doing things well; then we must show the correct ways if necessary, and positively guide them back to our standards.

Immediate positive corrective feedback is the on-the-spot evaluation and training we give employees to ensure that they are always doing everything the proper way. Feedback reinforces a desired behavior and corrects an undesirable behavior. For feedback to reinforce behavior, it must be in a language to which our employees can relate. "Nice job," can be reinforcing to one employee who responds to praise. However, another employee might find the praise patronizing and prefer instead a nod or an extra duty. We have to know our employees to know what they will respond to, and then adjust our responses accordingly to match their needs.

Some employees need more attention than others. Too much attention can annoy or insult some employees, while others might feel insecure with less attention. Our job is to get the most out of our employees. We first have to figure out how, and then do it. Our employees like to do good work and perform to their potentials. Management is far more than simply issuing orders. We are dealing with a diverse workforce, comprised of individuals brought up to expect a certain modicum of respect, appreciation, and fulfillment from their job. We can issue orders, but unless we are issuing them in ways our employees will respond to, they may not follow them (and they may go to work elsewhere).

If our job is to supervise employees, we must be on the floor where they are actually performing their work. We cannot be in an office somewhere. Supervision involves knowing our employees, having professional relationships with them, and communicating with them. Coaching is the name for this ongoing employee/supervisor interaction.

Counseling

Counseling is a one-on-one interview where a manager helps an employee seek solutions to his or her problems. After reading this chapter, a manager or future manager might ask in frustration, "What am I supposed to be—their mother?" The answer is, "Well, sort of!"

Authoritarian management was never very effective, but with today's competitive business environment and the characteristics of today's labor pool, authoritarian management simply does not work. We can stubbornly insist on managing in old-style ways, but we will have dissatisfied employees and customers, a high turnover rate, and day-to-day problems associated with poor management.

Management's job is to make an operation work. As managers, we have to do whatever it takes to reach that goal. Research and experience have shown that a caring, nurturing, team effort works better. While we all have similar emotions, feelings, and desires, we also are all unique. We have different personalities and combinations of personality traits. We will each have to develop a management style that works for us. This usually comes in time if we are paying attention to who we are and to those things that cause our employees to positively respond. No matter what management style we develop, this style must incorporate humanistic characteristics in order to be effective and acceptable to our employees.

People have always suffered from life's turns. Death, illness, alcoholism, and relationship problems have always been with us. Today, however, we are more attuned to life's problems and, perhaps, have more tools to deal with them. There are support groups for almost every tormenting situation we might find ourselves in, and misery does not discriminate. Divorce and cancer rates seem to be equally spread across socioeconomic lines. We, as managers, are just as likely to find ourselves dealing with these problems as any of our employees.

We are more understanding managers if we have already had our hearts broken. The pain of a manager's divorce is the same as the pain of a dishwasher's divorce. That sort of pain can get in the way of any employees doing their jobs. Life's problems seem to be rampant. Perhaps, it is because we no longer feel the need to suffer quietly. Whatever the reason, we, as managers, will have to deal with employees (or ourselves) as personal problems crop up. We can terminate an employee who is heartbroken and distracted by grief from one problem or another, but we will save nothing because the replacement will most likely be in a similar boat in the future. We all have problems, and they tend to interfere with our work.

All employees, including ourselves, must always meet certain standards. Personal problems are not acceptable excuses for not meeting these standards. Because an employee is a recovering alcoholic does not make it okay to go "off the wagon" and be intoxicated at work or be absent due to a hangover. If the unacceptable behavior continued, we obviously would have grounds to terminate the employee. It is, however, in our best interest to attempt to get the employee back on track rather than having to find and train another employee who also would most likely have problems. We achieve this through the counseling process.

Most of us are not qualified to practice psychotherapy. We are, however, qualified to recognize problems, express concern, and recommend professional help. Many companies have employee assistance programs to refer troubled employees to the appropriate agencies for help. We cannot afford to ignore problems if they are negatively affecting the employees' work or have the potential to negatively affect it. Bottom-line results require that we address problems. We have quite a bit of influence and power over our employees. With this influence and power comes responsibility to use it in their best interests. We will be better human beings and better managers if we take our responsibilities seriously.

Attitude changes, tardiness, absenteeism, sloppy work, and so forth can be indications of problems that may be interfering with the work of your employees. Employee appraisal, counseling, and progressive discipline are very similar. The same principles of fairness, privacy, and equity apply to all three. We might notice a negative change in an employee's attitude towards the job, coworkers, customers, and/or management. Initially, the attitude change could be addressed in a counseling manner. We would define what we see as the problem and what we would like to see changed, then arrange to discuss the problem with the employee in a private interview. All our motivational knowledge and communication skills would be employed in this interview to attempt to discover what is going on and how to change the worker's behavior back to acceptable.

Our purpose is to get the employee back on track and functioning up to our standards. As much as we care about our people, we are not, however, a social agency, and it must be made clear that the employee will have to meet certain standards or leave. We give them (and document) as much help as we possibly can. Most employees will get over their problems, and, with a little help from us, can again function acceptably in spite of them. In rare cases where the employee does not get back on track, we would move into a progressive discipline process.

It is a good idea for us to keep in mind that we could find ourselves in problems similar to those of our employees. We can ask ourselves questions, such as: How would I like my supervisor to handle a change in my own work behavior? Would I like intolerance or threats? Would intolerance or threats effectively solve the problem? Would handling the situation with intolerance and threats be good for the operation, for other workers, and for management?

We have to do what works. And intolerance and threats do not work.

CONCLUSION

Great training will not work by itself. We must hire workers who are willing and capable of doing the job and then train them. We cannot train incapable or unwilling workers to perform at necessary standards. The training will not be effective if it is not utilized properly by employees who have been trained to use the documents and deliver the training. Training alone will not ensure that employees meet certain standards after successfully completing it. Therefore, ongoing training or coaching is required to sustain the effort.

It is very time consuming and tedious to develop training documents. Collection of all the data necessary for the development of training documents could take days or weeks. None of it is difficult or hard to understand, it is simply time consuming and expensive. Once we have a well-designed training program implemented that is justified by a needs assessment up front and evaluated at the end, combined with good hiring and supervision practices, we will have more satisfied employees and customers, and our operation will run more efficiently with far fewer problems. It will be professionally managed.

KEY WORDS

Motivation	Coaching
Diversity	Reinforcement
Communication	Immediate Positive Corrective Feedback
Supervision	Counseling

CHAPTER THOUGHT QUESTIONS

1. Think about where you are in your life right now. Do you have your basic survival needs met? Are you fairly secure? Do you have friends and a network or two that you are a part of? What motivates you at work or at school? What are you willing to work for? Do you respond to more money, time off, social activities, or more responsibility and/or autonomy on the job? Please discuss where you are in your life and how that determines the incentives for which you are willing to work.

2. Think about other times in your life. Have you always been as secure or as connected to people as you may or may not be now? How have your needs changed as your life has changed? What incentives were you willing to work for when you were at a different place in your life? Discuss how these preferred incentives have changed as your life has changed.

3. Noting that your own needs have changed as your life has changed, discuss how you might recognize your workers' individual needs and determine the appropriate incentives for their particular needs. Why is it necessary for managers or trainers to do this in order to be effective?

4. Look at the circles of people you are part of—family, friends, people you work with, organizations you may be a part of, and so forth. In each circle, identify the elements of diversity (age, social class, religion, ethnic background, education, nationality, and so forth). Note and discuss the expanding range of diversity as the circles become less intimate. What does this mean to you in terms of management? Training design?

5. Describe a recent communication misunderstanding that you have had with a friend, relative, acquaintance, teacher, worker, or boss. What was the misunderstanding over? What was each person's version of the reason for the misunderstanding? How was the misunderstanding resolved? How could it have been avoided in the first place?

6. Describe the steps necessary for effective communication. Discuss why the steps are important and necessary in terms of diversity.

7. Describe coaching and compare and contrast it with the less effective authoritarian management style. Have you experienced both styles of supervision? Which did you prefer and why?

8. Reinforcement and immediate positive corrective feedback are the tools we use in coaching to observe, praise, and correct. Please define and describe these two tools and discuss their importance and use in terms of diversity and communication.

9. Have you experienced any tragedies or serious troubles in your life yet—death of a loved one, divorce, illness, or addiction? Think about how you felt at the time and how it affected your interest and ability to do your work or take an active part in your normal activities. How likely is it that you will again be faced with another of life's unpleasant surprises? How likely is it that people on your staff will have things like this happen? Discuss why you should be compassionate.

10. Describe the counseling process and discuss how and why managers should try to get troubled employees back on track. Include performance standards in your discussion.

14 Costing the Training Program

OBJECTIVES

The purpose of this chapter is to take a closer look at how we determine the costs of training design, whether it be for single positions or an entire program.

Upon completion of Chapter 14, the student should be able to

- Discuss why it is important to determine the costs of training design.
- Determine the cost of designing training for a position or an entire program.

Cost Determination Before or After

When we undertake the design of training (for either a position or an entire program), we may need to provide a cost estimate. This is a rather difficult task, especially when tackled the first time. It is far easier to categorize and tally costs as we go through the design process. We have repeatedly said that designing instruction or training is expensive. We would not want to go through the design process and find, at the end, that we have spent more money than we have . . . or more than the training is actually worth in terms of the initial problem it was designed to solve.

Hospitality Training Design (the imaginary firm contracted by The Garden Terrace Inn (GTI) in our Chapter Three case study) gave the General Manager (GM) a very close estimate of the total cost for training design. Unless money is no object, an up-front cost estimate is essential to avoid unpleasant surprises when it comes time to pay the bill. Hospitality Training Design has designed many training programs and knows how long it takes and the costs for each step of the process. If this is our first foray into formal training design, though, we will have no way of knowing in advance what these costs will be.

We are, instead, going to record costs as they occur and tally them up at the end of the design process. In doing so, we will be better able to realistically estimate the cost of subsequent training design in advance of the process. Again, there is no formula for determining the cost of the training design. It takes careful accounting and experience. If we wanted to become independent training designers, it would be a good idea to design the training for ourselves first. Within a secure management position, we could get a feel for the time and expenses involved before setting ourselves up as outside consultants. Without this exercise, we might be giving up-front estimates only to realize later that it actually cost us money to do the job.

Cost of Training Design versus Cost of Training

The cost of designing the training is basically a one-time expense. Once the training is designed, we will use these documents over and over. The cost of providing the training is ongoing and will vary, depending on how many people are being trained, their initial skill levels, and so on. The cost of training design must be factored into the cost of the training program. However, each time the training is utilized, the cost per trainee is reduced as it is spread over more people.

Cost of Training Design

To determine the cost of designing training, we have to categorize and tally every minute we, or others, spend on each component of the Training Design Model. Then, we need to multiply the hours spent on the project by the pay rate for each person. We have to keep track of all the costs for paper, printing, office supplies, and materials throughout the design process. The following Cost Analysis Form itemizes cost considerations for the various components of the Training Design Model with spaces for documentation and totals.

Cost Analysis Form

Training Design for ————————————————————
(name of position or program)

For all components of the Training Design Model, always consider

- Cost of paper, printer, secretarial, research
- Total hours of anyone's work on all components of the model
- Any additional considerations noted in the following section for each component
- Any other expenses that are not noted here

Training Design Model Component	Materials and Supplies	Hours and Cost per hr.	Cost
Construct Needs Assessment Plan	$	# @	$

Design surveys and interview questions to find out the organization's and individual's needs.

- Pilot test costs
- Costs to duplicate, disseminate, administer, and analyze
- Time spent being interviewed or filling out surveys

Develop script to reassure employees.

- Pilot test or practice
- Time of employees to listen to the script

Design surveys and interview questions to find out the position needs.

- Pilot test costs
- Costs to duplicate, disseminate, administer, and analyze
- Time spent being interviewed or filling out surveys

Develop an observation checklist.

- Pilot test costs
- Time spent observing and using the checklist
- Cost of analyzing the observation

Training Design Model Component	Materials and Supplies	Hours and Cost per hr.	Cost
Write a job list.			
Do task analysis for each item on job list.			
• Cost of any additional employee time that might be incurred while doing a task analysis			
Categorize a job list and a task analysis.			
• Cost of any other employee input necessary to check for validity			
Determine the training methods for various categories and/or tasks.			
Devise a training plan.			
Write the lesson plans.			
Select a trainer.			
Do a task analysis.			
Devise a training plan for training the trainer.			
Write lesson plans for training the trainer.			
Construct evaluation plans and instruments (tests) for all four levels of evaluation.			
• Cost of pilot testing			
• Employee time taking tests and answering evaluation questions			
• Cost of analyzing the results			
List any other costs incurred to design the training.			
Complete the Cost Analysis Form.			
TOTALS			$

Cost of Training

Determining what it costs to deliver the training each time is vital information but it is not the focus of this chapter. Whenever training is delivered, a trainer must be paid, the trainee must be paid, and there also may be a reduction in the trainer's production that would have to be picked up by another employee or in overtime. There may be costs for the duplication of training materials, samples (such as prepared menu items to taste), supplies (such as ingredients used to practice with), and/or energy costs. There may be additional maintenance and administrative costs. All these figures must be categorized and tallied to determine the total cost of delivering the training. Using these figures, we can factor in the cost of training design and arrive at a total cost for the program.

Finally, using the total cost figure, we then can determine the cost per trainee by dividing the total cost by the number of trainees per year.

$$\text{Cost per trainee} = \frac{\text{total cost of training program}}{\text{number of trainees per year}}$$

It stands to reason that the more trainees who go through the program, the less it costs per trainee. As we said earlier, we would not go to the effort and expense of designing formal training if we were only going to train one employee.

The Garden Terrace Inn: Determining the Cost of Training Design

The initial interview with the GM (conducted to determine organization needs) indicated that training was to be designed for the line positions of cook, dishwasher, housekeeper, front desk personnel, night auditor, and server. We are going to categorize and tally the costs for one small portion of the entire training design project for GTI. We will look at Chapters Five and Six and figure out the cost for designing the surveys and interview questions to find the position needs, writing the job list, and doing task analysis for just one duty on the cook position's job list. (It would be useful to review Chapters Five and Six before continuing.)

Cost Analysis Form

Training Design for ———— Cook (one small portion of the position) ————

(name of position or program)

Training Design Model Component	Materials and Supplies	Hours and Cost per hr.	Cost
Obtain the cook's job description. Check with Chef Paul to see if the job description is accurate and up to date.			
Devise questions for the cook to result in a job list.			
Interview one cook in depth for a job list and a task analysis. (Andi 3+ hrs. @ $10/hr.)		Cook 4 Designer 4	40
Check the interview results (job list) with chef and sous chef to see if they are accurate, then reconcile any discrepancies.		Chef Sous Designer	
Categorize the job list.		Designer 1	
Devise an observation checklist from the task analysis form. (Cut steaks, medallions, and brochettes)		Designer	
Conduct an observation to note and reconcile discrepancies.		Designer 1	
Totals			**$40**

Pay per hour:

Cook	$10
Sous Chef	$15
Chef	$25

The cost of planning and implementing a job analysis for just one duty of one position came to $40 without including the designer's time. The interview questions were already developed and just reconsidered by the designer. While the cook's position has a total of 48 duties, they were all addressed in the four-hour cook interview. Many have to do with following recipes, so there will be no need for a task analysis. In addition, there were costs to do the initial needs assessment planning and implementation. There also will be costs to devise the training plan and considerable costs to write the lesson plans, evaluation instruments, and training for the trainer.

The designer in this case study spent a little less than seven hours on this portion of the design process. Designers generally do not work by the hour, but rather for a fee for the entire project. We would have to add the cost of the seven hours to the $40. For a manager or training designer, the cost would be at least $140 (most likely a whole lot more). Managers who choose to design their own training add training design responsibilities to their existing duties. Because there are only so many hours in a day, they are forced to spend less time on their primary responsibilities. The duties that are sacrificed are generally supervisory in nature, and that can be a very costly sacrifice in terms of customer and employee satisfaction. We would continue categorizing and tallying hours and costs every step through the training design model. It is obvious that the final cost could be considerable.

CONCLUSION

This textbook was not developed to prepare people for professional instructional designer consulting careers. It was, instead, developed to enable managers to design their own training. While training design is not difficult, it is tedious and expensive to do. It also is an extremely valuable, rare, and sought after skill to have. While we may need to design whole training programs, more often we will be designing small pieces of training or training for just one position. If an organization has been getting along without training, it may be less of a drain financially to design one position after another until an entire program is in place.

Well-designed training is a necessity in today's competitive business environment. Large hospitality chains may have instructional designers on staff to provide formal training documents for all their operations. Independents can hire training design consultants or design the training themselves. Training design is a learned skill, though, and hopefully it is now a part of your inventory.

Glossary

B

Behavioral Objective—In training objectives, the objectives state what the employee will be able to do upon completion of the training.

Body Mechanics—The science dealing with body forces and motions.

C

Closed Questions—Questions with specific answer options.

Coaching—The act of monitoring, praising, and positively correcting an employee's performance.

D

Demonstration—It occurs during training when the trainer actually performs the task for the learner while explaining all steps.

Diversity—The human characteristics that make people different from one another.

Dovetailing—The process wherein the steps of a duty are fit closely together to avoid a waste of motion.

Duty—One specific task an employee does that is part of their job.

E

Employee Appraisal—A formal, periodic interview with individual employees to discuss their specific job performance strengths and weaknesses for the purpose of improving their performance.

Evaluation—The utilization of research methods after training to determine if the training was effective.

F

Formal Training—A structured form of training following a predetermined plan of instruction.

G

Group Training—Training more than one employee at the same time to do the same task.

I

Illiteracy—The state of being unable to read or write.

Immediate Positive Corrective Feedback—Watching employees try something they were just shown, and coaching them through it to ensure that they did it correctly.

Individual Needs—The knowledge, skills, attitudes, and motivations a person brings to a prospective position of employment.

Informal Training—Training where there is no predetermined, written plan.

Instructional Design—The systematic development of materials and methods for teaching a specific body of knowledge.

Interview—A face-to-face verbal question and answer interaction between an interviewer and a respondent.

J

Job Analysis—The rigorous research process used to update or write accurate job descriptions and specifications.

Job Description—A description of the position and main duties a person will be required to perform after the training.

Job List—An identification of all the duties for a specific position.

Job Specification—A description of the characteristics, skills, education, and experience a prospective employee needs to fulfill a job's requirements.

L

Lecture—A semi-formal presentation by a teacher or trainer verbally telling students or trainees about something.

Lesson Plan—A script of the training with all the materials, activities, and instructions needed to meet the training objectives.

M

Marketing—The identification of customers and the development of products, pricing, and distribution aimed at satisfying their needs and wants.

Motion Economy—In physical work, it is the avoidance of repetitive or needless motion through the proper structuring of tasks.

N

Needs Assessment—The systematic process used to collect appropriate data in order to determine the precise problem and whether training is a good fix.

O

Objectives—Statements of what trainees will be able to do upon completion of their training.

Objectivity—With respect to testing, objectivity ensures that a test does not leave anything up to guesswork or interpretation.

Observation Checklist—A list of sequential duties used during an observation to determine if an employee is doing the job as per the organizational standards and how they, themselves, described their duties in a previous interview.

On-the-job Training—Planned, structured training conducted on the actual job site with written objectives, content, and procedures.

Open Questions—Questions that do not give specific answer options.

Organizational Needs—An organization's mission, philosophy, and goals, and how these items determine an organization's search for employees.

Orientation—The process where a business welcomes and introduces new employees to their business.

P

Performance Standard—A standard defining precisely how a duty should be performed and/or how it should look when completed.

Pilot Test—In a questionnaire design, it is a dry run on smaller groups resembling the people for which the questionnaire was designed.

Position Needs—The required behaviors for a job that are determined through a task analysis.

Practicality—With respect to testing, practicality is attained when tests are kept simple and to the point of the objective, and when they are clear and easy to administer and grade.

Psycho-motor—A type of muscular activity required to execute and achieve a particular result.

Q

Questionnaire—A written form containing questions and answer options that is administered verbally or in writing.

R

Recruiting—The active search for employees with the characteristics and/or skills necessary to do the job.

Reliability—With respect to testing, reliability ensures that a test measures the same thing the same way each time.

Role-play—Instructional method enabling trainees to act out situations under a trainer's direction.

S

Segment—A smaller division of the market consisting of people with similar product needs based on commonalities such as age, interests, or lifestyles.

Selection—A process of reviewing applications and conducting interviews to determine which prospective employee best matches a job specification.

Self-instructional Method—A structured lesson or lessons that trainees can follow themselves.

Simulation—A contrived situation that resembles a real situation where trainees can safely practice and hone their new service skills before dealing with the public.

Standard—A clear, concise description of the way something is to be or is to be done.

Structured Interview—An interview with a structured list of questions.

Supervision—The ongoing day-to-day monitoring of an employees' performance with reinforcement and positive feedback to maintain the standards achieved in training.

T

Target Market—A specific group of individuals at which a business aims its marketing.

Task—One specific step in a duty.

Task Analysis—A process where a particular task or duty is broken down into separate steps.

Team—A group working together toward a common goal.

Training—The process used for the development of knowledge and skills necessary to perform the jobs, duties, and tasks found in an organization.

Training Design—Instructional design aimed at teaching a person to do a specific job.

Training Design Model—A comprehensive program for training that is made up of seven interrelated components.

Training Plan—A well-thought-out, written plan detailing training topics and a schedule of when, where, and by whom they will be presented.

Triangulation—The process of collecting the same information from different sources and in different ways.

Turnover—The rate at which businesses replace workers.

U

Unstructured Interview—An interview without a structured list of questions.

V

Validity—With respect to testing, validity ensures that a test measures what it was supposed to measure.

W

Work Simplification—The study of duties and tasks to determine the most efficient methods of performance.

Index

absenteeism, 27
adult learning principles, 82–95
age of workforce, 6
appraisals, 11–12
authoritarian management, 21, 185

before or after cost determination, 190–191
behavioral objectives, 99, 130–131
body mechanics studies, 59
breaking down steps in task analysis, 74–76

career ladders, 29
categorization of job list, 71–73
changes, needs analysis and, 34
chronic unemployment, 7
classroom training methods, 5, 89–90
closed questions, in questionnaires, 44
coaching, 20–21, 184–185
common sense in needs assessment, 31
communication skills, 181–184
community-related training programs, 7
competition among trainees, 83
competitive advantage, 2–3, 8–9, 12
consistency of service, 2
cost of training, 175–176, 190–196
counseling, 20–21, 185–187
critique form, 162–163, 174
culture (*See* diversity of workforce)
customizing instruction, 5

damage, 28
data collection methods, 35, 38
defining trainees, 96–98, 149
demonstrations, 18, 84, 86–87, 162–163
design model for training, 15–26, 130, 147
   case study in, 21–25
   coaching and counseling in, 20–21,
      178–189

components and steps of, with human
   resources model, 16
evaluation of training in, 20, 165–177
implementation of training in, 20, 165–177
lesson plans in, 18–19, 112
"model" defined for, 16
needs assessment in, 17, 20, 27–40
objectives statements in, 17
organizational charts in, 22–23
standards in, 19
summary of model for, 24–25
topics to be covered in, 18
training plan or schedule in, 17–18, 96
Dictionary of Occupational Titles, 31
disabled employee training, 133–134
discovery method of learning, 85–86
discrimination, 96–97
diversity of workforce, 6–7, 132–133, 180–181
dovetailing of steps/tasks, 60
duties, 55–57, 62, 98

economic cycle, needs analysis and, 34, 38
education and experience assessment, 62, 98
elderly in workforce, 6
employee acceptance of training, 168–169
employee appraisals, 11–12
employee incentive programs, 137, 139–140
employee input, in needs analysis and,
      32–33, 50
employee meetings, 30, 135–136
encouragement, 83
English as second language, 7, 173
ethnic diversity (*See* diversity of workforce)
evaluation of training, 20, 165–177
   cost of training and, 175–176, 190–196
   critique form for, 174
   employee acceptance of training and,
      168–169

feedback and, 167–168
four levels of, 168–170
instruments used in, 171–172
level one, 171–172
level two, 173
level three, 174–175
level four, 175
mastering training in, 166–168
objectivity of, 170
practicality of, 170
pre- and post-training comparison in,
    169, 175
questionnaires for, 173
reliability and validity of test instruments
    in, 170
subject matter and topic of training in,
    169, 174–175
tests, test criteria in, 170, 172–173
training documents utilized in, 166
exercises, 5
existing documents, 35, 61

facilities assessment, 33
feedback, 20, 84, 167–168, 184–185
follow around training (*See also* shadowing),
    85
formal training, 4–6, 10, 15

generalization of employees, 96–97
grades, 18–19
group dynamics, 134–136
group training, 129–144
    behavioral objectives in, 130–131
    case study in, 136–143
    design of, 136–143
    design of training model and, 130
    disabled employees and, 133–134
    diversity of employees in, 132–133
    employee incentive programs and, 137,
        139–140
    group dynamics and team building in,
        134–136
    instruction design and, 130–131
    lectures in, 137
    lesson plans in, 140–143
    objectives in, 130–131
    reward systems and, 137, 139–140
    task analysis for, 137–138
    training methods for, 131–132

hand-outs, 5
hands-on learning, 4, 84
hiring practices, 97
homeless as workforce, 7
human resources, 10–12, 16, 30, 54–66,
    96–97, 186–187

illiteracy in workforce, 6–7
image, 3
immigrant workforce, 7
implementation of training, 20, 165–177
individual needs, 28–29, 34, 37, 46–47
industry-related training programs, 7
informal training, 4–6
instructional design, 5–6, 44–45, 54–60, 67,
    130–131
instrument development, 41, 171–172
interviewing new employees, 10–11
interviews in needs analysis, 35, 42–44,
    61–64
introduction to training, 1–14
    formal vs. informal training in, 4–6, 10
    human resources management review and,
        10–12
    marketing and standards in, 7–9
    process of training in, 2
    turnover rates and, 3
    workforce diversity and, 6–7

job analysis, 10–12, 30, 54–67, 73–79, 98
    case study in, 61–64
    categorization of job list and, 71–73
    duties vs. tasks in, 55–57, 62
    education and experience assessment for,
        62, 98
    existing documents in, 61
    implementing of, 67–81
    instructional design and, 54–60
    interviews and questionnaires in,
        61–64
    job descriptions in, 61
    job lists in, 55–57, 67–73
    observation checklists in, 64, 78
    performance standards and, 57, 67
    pilot testing instructions in, 76
    training design and, 54–55, 61
    work simplification and motion economy
        in, 58–60, 67
job descriptions, 10, 61, 98, 150

job lists, 55–57, 67–73, 148–149
job specifications, 10, 97, 150

knowledge, skills, abilities assessment, 62, 98

labor pool, 7, 34, 38
learning styles, 17, 82–83
lectures, 5, 18, 84–85, 88, 137
length of training sessions, 84
lesson plans, 18–19, 112–128, 140–143, 166
    design of training model and, 112
    on the job training (OJT) and, 113–126
    training the trainer and, 148, 151–162
levels of evaluation, 168–175
long-term goals, 28

management styles and training, 5–6, 21,
    185–186
management support, for needs analysis,
    33–34
marketing and standards, 7–9
morale, 21, 27
motion economy, 58–60, 67
motivation, 178–180

National Council on Vocational Education, 31
needs assessment, 20, 27–40, 50–52
    case study in, 36–39, 50–52
    changes and, 34
    common sense in, 31–32
    data collection methods for, 35, 38
    data processed for, 33
    design model for training and, 17, 33
    employee input in, 32–33, 50
    employee meetings in, 30
    existing documents in, 31, 35
    facilities assessment in, 33
    implementing of, 41–53
    individual needs in, 28–29, 34, 37, 46–47
    instrument development for, 41
    interviews and questionnaires for, 42–50
    labor, economic cycle, population data in,
        34, 38
    long-term goals and, 28
    management support and, 33–34
    methods for, 29–30
    new operations and, 30
    ongoing nature of, 32–33
    organizational needs in, 29–30, 34, 36–37

    planning considerations in, 27–28, 33–35
    position needs in, 29, 35, 37
    script development for, 41
    task analysis in, 29, 41
    technology assessment in, 34
    training the trainer and, 148–149

objectives of training, 17, 99–102, 130–131,
    167–168
objectivity of evaluation, 170
observation checklists, job analysis and, 64, 78
on the job training (OJT), 90, 103, 113–126
open questions, in interviews, 42
organizational charts, 22–23
organizational needs, 29–30, 34, 36–37
orientation for new employees, 11

performance standards, 57, 67
personal problems, 186–187
pilot testing instructions, 76
pilot testing questionnaires, 44–45
population data, needs analysis and, 34, 38
position needs, 29, 35
positive feedback (*See also* feedback),
    167–168, 184–185
practicality of evaluation, 170
praising, 184–185
pre- and post-training comparison, in evalua-
    tion, 169, 175
prepared training materials, 90
preparing employees for needs assessment, 50
problem solving, 21
productivity, 21, 28, 58–60, 67
profiles, training, 98–99
psycho-motor activities, 86–87

quality of training, 4
questionnaires, 44–50, 61, 173

recruiting new employees, 10
reinforcement, 20
reliability of test instruments, 170
reward systems, 137, 139–140, 178–180
role playing, 5, 88

sanitation, 70
schedule of training, 104–109
scope of training, 27
script development, needs analysis and, 41

segmentation of market, 9
selecting trainers, 102–104, 146–147
self-instructional activities, 89
service industry and training, 2
shadowing, 4–5, 85
simulations, 87–88, 172
standards, 9, 19–21, 57
steps in training design model, 16
structured interviews, 42
supervision, 11, 20–21, 184–187
surveys (*See also* questionnaires), 35, 44

targeting of markets, 9
task analysis, 29, 41, 67, 73–79, 137–138
tasks, 55–57, 62
team-building, 134–136
technology assessment, 34
technology of training, 5
terminating employees, 186
tests, test criteria, 170, 172–173
topics of training, 18, 99–102, 150–151, 169, 174–175
trained to train trainers, 4
trainees, defining, 96–98, 149
trainers, 102–104, 146–147, 166–168
training design, 54–55, 61, 191–194
training materials, 90
training methods and adult learning principles, 82–95, 129–144
   case study in, 90–93
   classroom methods in, 89–90
   demonstrations in, 84, 86–87
   discovery method in, 85–86
   hands-on training in, 84
   lectures in, 84–85, 88
   on the job training (OTJ) in, 90, 103
   prepared training materials for, 90
   psycho-motor activities and, 86–87
   role plays in, 88
   self-instructional activities in, 89
   simulations in, 87–88
training plan or schedule, 17–18, 96–111
   behavioral objectives in, 99
   defining trainees for, 96–98
   design of training model and, 96
   discrimination and generalizations in, avoiding, 96–97
   duties vs. tasks in, 98
   education and experience assessment for, 98
   job description in, 98
   job specifications in, 97
   knowledge, skills, and abilities assessment for, 98
   objectives of training in, 99–102
   schedule of training in, 104–109
   trainer selection in, 102–104
   training profiles for, 98–99
   training the trainer and, 148
   training topics in, 99–102
training profiles, 98–99
training the trainer, 5, 19, 145–164
   characteristics of trainers and, 146–147
   defining trainees for, 149
   demonstration critique form for, 162–163
   design of training model and, 147
   designing instruction for, 147–148
   job lists in, 148–149
   job specification and job descriptions in, 150
   lesson plans and, 148, 151–162
   needs assessment in, 148–149
   selecting a trainer, 146–147
   topic of training for, 150–151
   training plans for, 148
triangulation, 30
turnover rates, 3, 27

uncontrollable variables, marketing and, 9
unskilled labor, 6
unstructured interviews, 42
upgrading equipment, 28

validity of test instruments, 170
Vocational-Technical Education Consortium of States, 31
Vocational Education Services, 31

waste, 28
women in workforce, 6
work simplification, 58–60, 67
workbooks, 89
workforce diversity (*See* diversity of workforce)